Praise for *The Ten Basic Principles of Good Parenting*

"[Steinberg] distills decades of research into a simple guide for moms and dads in the trenches. . . . No parent is perfect, but Steinberg's book can help moms and dads bring up their own grades."

—*Newsweek*

"Steinberg offers sage advice as well as pragmatic steps to follow, in the hopes that you can learn to become a more 'mindful' parent."

—*The Boston Globe*

"A blueprint on how to be the best parent for your child."

—*The San Diego Union-Tribune*

"A real gem from one of the world's most trusted psychologists! In this easy-to-read little book, Professor Steinberg crystallizes what science tells us about how to raise children. Chock-full of examples and solutions, this is a must-read for parents and parents-to-be!"

—Kathy Hirsh-Pasek, Professor of Psychology, Temple University, and author of *How Babies Talk* and *Einstein Never Used Flashcards*

"Dr. Steinberg's prescriptions are grounded in science, and there is a note in his writing of something less quantifiable and perhaps even more valuable: wisdom."

—Robert Needlman, M.D., Associate Professor of Pediatrics, Case Western Reserve University; *Dr. Spock's Baby and Childcare* (8th edition), updated and revised by Robert Needlman, M.D.

"Larry Steinberg gets it right! In this brief but information-packed book, he helps parents apply the science of child development to their relationships with their children. It is warm, insightful, and eminently practical."

—Lawrence Kutner, Ph.D., Codirector, Harvard Medical School Center for Mental Health and Media

"A powerful argument for the importance of parents in shaping emotionally healthy children. Steinberg's philosophy is based on decades of scientific research in the parenting field, and rests on ten main beliefs that span childhood from infancy to adolescence. . . . Brims with potent messages about the importance and responsibility of good parenting, providing useful guidelines for new parents and a valuable refresher course for veterans."

—*Publishers Weekly*

ALSO BY LAURENCE STEINBERG

Beyond the Classroom:
Why School Reform Has Failed and What Parents Need to Do

Crossing Paths:
How Your Child's Adolescence Triggers Your Own Crisis
(with Wendy Steinberg)

When Teenagers Work:
The Psychological and Social Costs of Adolescent Employment
(with Ellen Greenberger)

You and Your Adolescent:
A Parent's Guide for Ages 10–20
(with Ann Levine)

The Ten Basic Principles
of Good Parenting

Laurence Steinberg, Ph.D.

SIMON & SCHUSTER PAPERBACKS

New York London Toronto Sydney

SIMON & SCHUSTER PAPERBACKS
Rockefeller Center
1230 Avenue of the Americas
New York, NY 10020

Copyright © 2004 by Laurence Steinberg

All rights reserved,
including the right of reproduction
in whole or in part in any form.

First Simon & Schuster trade paperback edition 2005

SIMON & SCHUSTER PAPERBACKS and colophon are registered trademarks
of Simon & Schuster, Inc.

For information regarding special discounts for bulk purchases,
please contact Simon & Schuster Special Sales:
1-800-456-6798 or business@simonandschuster.com

Manufactured in the United States of America

7   9   10   8   6

The Library of Congress has cataloged the hardcover edition as follows:

Steinberg, Laurence D., 1952–
The ten basic principles of good parenting / Laurence Steinberg.
p.   cm.
Includes index.
1. Parenting. 2. Parent and child. I. Title.
HQ755.8.S75 2004
649'.1—dc22
2003067380

ISBN 0-7432-5115-6
ISBN 0-7432-5116-4 (Pbk)

Acknowledgments

It is a pleasure to thank several people whose encouragement, support, and advice shaped this book in important ways.

At the top of my list is my wife, Wendy. Anyone setting out to write a book on parenting could not be luckier than to be married to someone who is not only a remarkable parent and a supportive spouse, but who also happens to be a talented writer and a meticulous editor. Wendy read and commented on every single page of this book, and both its substance and style are far superior as a result.

Writing this book was something I had wanted to do for several years, but I would not have actually taken the project on had it not been for the encouragement of my good friends Felecia and Jeff Weiss; my agent, Virginia Barber; and my editor, Bob Bender.

I am especially indebted to Kathy Hirsh-Pasek and Anne Fletcher, both of whom are wise parents and accomplished developmental psychologists. They each read major portions of the manuscript and made important and much-appreciated suggestions. I also bounced many of the ideas in this book off our son, Ben, who is now a young adult, and he was exceptionally helpful in making me see what was important and what was not. I suppose that's what children are for.

The basic ideas contained in this book are based on the work of many colleagues who have devoted their careers to the scientific study of children and families. It is impossible to list all of those whose seminal research on parenting has shown that what parents do really does make a difference, but I must mention four specific luminaries whose work has been a model for my own and whose important discoveries are reflected in the ten principles of good parenting discussed in this book: Diana Baumrind of the University of California, Berkeley; Urie Bronfenbrenner of Cornell University; E. Mavis Hetherington of the University of Virginia; and Eleanor Maccoby of Stanford University. It has been a privilege to know and be influenced by each of them.

Finally, a special note of thanks to the colleagues with whom I've studied parents and children. Much of the original research that informs this book has been conducted by other experts, but a lot of it comes from the studies that I have done on parent-child relationships at Cornell University; the University of California, Irvine; the University of Wisconsin; and Temple University over the past thirty years with some wonderful collaborators and students. I am particularly grateful to Shelli Avenevoli, Brad Brown, Beth Cauffman, Nancy Darling, Sandy Dornbusch, Julie Elmen, Anne Fletcher, Marjory Roberts Gray, Ellen Greenberger, John Hill, Susan Silverberg Koerner, Susie Lamborn, Amanda Morris, Nina Mounts, Fran Sessa, and Jennifer Silk. I hope I got it right.

For Wendy and Ben

The Ten Basic Principles of Good Parenting

1. What You Do Matters

2. You Cannot Be Too Loving

3. Be Involved in Your Child's Life

4. Adapt Your Parenting to Fit Your Child

5. Establish Rules and Set Limits

6. Help Foster Your Child's Independence

7. Be Consistent

8. Avoid Harsh Discipline

9. Explain Your Rules and Decisions

10. Treat Your Child with Respect

Contents

Being a Better Parent

WHEN PEOPLE find out that I'm both a parent and a psychologist who has spent his entire career studying parenting, I'm often asked whether what I've learned as a researcher has helped me to be a better parent. The answer is that of course it has. It's like asking a professional chef whether studying cooking for a living has made him or her better in the kitchen at home. How could it not? Like anything else, good parenting requires knowledge.

I've studied parents and their children for well over twenty-five years. I've published several books and hundreds of articles on parenting and child development, and I've been the editor in charge of articles on parent-child relationships for the most prestigious scientific journal in the field of child psychology. My own instincts as a parent have been shaped by what I've devoted my career to studying, and when I've had doubts or questions about what to do as a parent—as all parents, even experts, invariably do—I have always regained my bearings by thinking about what I've learned from the thousands of families I've studied and the thousands of research reports I've read.

In this book, I'm going to share this understanding with you.

This book is different from other books on parenting because it is based on the science of good parenting, on literally thousands of well-designed research studies—research that is just as credible as

2 • The Ten Basic Principles of Good Parenting

the research that scientists use to test new drugs, design safer automobiles, and construct sturdier buildings. Unlike most other parenting books on the market, this one is not based on one person's opinion, or someone's experiences in raising a couple of children, or the observations somebody made over the course of working with a few dozen families in a clinical practice. The advice contained in this book is based on what scientists who study parenting have learned from decades of systematic research involving hundreds of thousands of families. What I've done is to synthesize and communicate what the experts have learned in a language that nonexperts can understand. I've boiled this knowledge down into ten basic principles.

This book is not about the nuts and bolts of parenting; it is not about how to feed, dress, teach, stimulate, or play with your child. There are many excellent books on the market that cover these topics comprehensively, written for parents with children of different ages.

This book is more about the philosophy of good parenting. It describes an approach to parenting that cuts across different issues and different age periods. What you'll learn is a general orientation to raising children that is grounded in the most accurate and up-to-date scientific information available.

Raising children is not typically something we think of as especially scientific. It may surprise you to learn, though, that there *is* a science of effective parenting and that there is an awful lot more systematic research on parenting than on many other aspects of life where we routinely rely on science to guide us. In fact, child psychologists and other experts have been studying parenting for about seventy-five years, and it is one of the most well-researched areas in the entire field of social science.

More important, the study of parenting is an area of research in which the findings are remarkably consistent, and where the findings have *remained* remarkably consistent over time. It's hard to think of many areas of research about which we can say that.

Guidance about what we should eat, how frequently we should exercise, or how we should cope with stress changes constantly. New medical treatments are invented all the time. Today's health advice contradicts what we heard just yesterday. But the scientific principles of good parenting have not changed one bit in close to forty years. In fact, the scientific evidence linking certain basic principles of parenting to healthy child development is so clear and so consistent that we can confidently say we know what works and what does not. If it seems that the advice given in popular books is inconsistent, it's because few popular books are grounded in well-documented science.

For the most part, parenting is something we just *do*, without really giving it much thought. Much of the time we don't stop and think about what we do as parents because circumstances don't permit us to. When you are scurrying around in the morning trying to find your children's homework before sending them off to school, or breaking up a fight between an older child and younger sibling who are going at each other in the backseat of the car, or trying to soothe a colicky infant when your head is pounding because the baby has been crying uninterrupted for the past half hour, you don't have the luxury of stopping and thinking about what the best approach might be. There are plenty of times when, as parents, all we *can* do is just react. This part of parenting will never change. A lot of parenting is driven by our instincts, our gut responses. But the truth is that some parents have better instincts than others. With a better understanding of what works when you parent, and why, and with enough practice, your instincts will get better.

There are plenty of situations where you *do* have time to think before you parent, though. When you are putting your preschooler to bed the night before the first day of school. When your third-grader hands you a terrific report card. When your seventh-grader is upset because her friends have jilted her. When your teenager comes home later than your agreed-upon curfew.

At these moments, you have time to stop and think through what you should do before you act, and your actions should be guided by the best information on how to handle the situation most effectively. The more you practice good parenting when you *do* have time to think before you act, the more natural good parenting will become during those moments when you are responding instinctively.

One of the most encouraging findings from research on children's development is that the fundamentals of good parenting are the same regardless of whether your child is male or female, six or sixteen, an only child, a twin, or a child with multiple siblings. They are the same regardless of whether the primary parent is a mother, a father, or some other caregiver. The basic principles of good parenting have been corroborated in studies done in different parts of the world, with different ethnic and racial groups, in poor as well as in rich families, and in families with divorced, separated, and married parents. The same principles hold true whether you are a biological parent, an adoptive parent, or a foster parent. They apply to parents with average children and to those with children who have special needs. They even hold true for individuals who work with children, like teachers, coaches, and mentors. The evidence is that strong.

People define good parenting in different ways, so let me get right to the point about my own definition. In my view, good parenting is parenting that fosters psychological adjustment—elements like honesty, empathy, self-reliance, kindness, cooperation, self-control, and cheerfulness. Good parenting is parenting that helps children succeed in school; it promotes the development of intellectual curiosity, motivation to learn, and desire to achieve. Good parenting is parenting that deters children from antisocial behavior, delinquency, and drug and alcohol use. Good parenting is parenting that helps protect children against the development of anxiety, depression, eating disorders, and other types of psychological distress.

I realize that my way of defining good parenting assumes that certain traits in children are more desirable than others. True enough. But in my experience, most parents want the things that the sort of parenting described in this book helps to promote. Parents from all walks of life want their children to be happy, responsible, scholastically successful, socially accepted, and well behaved. But they all don't necessarily know how to achieve these goals.

I can't guarantee that if you follow the principles set out in this book your child will never have any problems, never fail a test in school, or never get into trouble, and any author of a book on parenting who makes such a promise should be distrusted. Children are influenced by many forces other than their parents, including their genetic makeup, their siblings, their friends, their school, the adults they encounter outside the family, and the mass media.

But what I *can* guarantee is that children raised according to the ten principles I discuss in this book are far more likely to develop in healthy ways and far less likely to develop difficulties than children who are raised in a different fashion. This is not an opinion. This is a fact, and there is a lot of strong evidence to back it up.

The ten principles of effective parenting discussed in this book are general ones that apply across the whole span of childhood and adolescence, although naturally some are more important than others during certain developmental periods. And, of course, the way these principles are applied will differ depending on the age of your child. For instance, it is important to be physically affectionate toward your child at all ages, but the ways you might express physical affection toward a toddler (holding your child in your lap while reading a book together) are not the same as the ways you might do so toward a teenager (giving your child a quick hug before she leaves on her first date). Similarly, whereas one of the principles calls for providing structure and limits, which is important at all ages, the sorts of limits you would place on a toddler (for example, never to cross the street without holding your hand) would clearly not be appropriate for an adolescent. Nevertheless, the overarching approach to parenting described in this book is applicable to families with children of all ages.

Trying to articulate a set of basic principles for effective parenting with children of all ages requires speaking in generalities rather than specifics, and no doubt there will be readers who see the ten principles as little more than common sense. But although the principles certainly make sense, their use is anything but common. In fact, many parents violate them all the time. One principle discourages the use of harsh punishment, for example, but if you've ever set foot in a shopping mall or supermarket, you've probably seen plenty of parents slap and scream at their children. Another principle advocates setting limits on children's behavior, but we all know parents who let their children run wild. A third encourages parents to treat their children with respect, but we've all heard parents speak to their children in a way that was nasty or dismissive. Just because something is sensible doesn't necessarily mean that it's common.

Most parents are pretty good parents. My aim in writing this book is to help parents, even pretty good parents, do a better job than they are currently doing. I've written it as much for parents who are just starting out as I have for parents whose children are well into adolescence. And I've written it just as much for parents who think they are good parents (and who may, in fact, *be* good parents) as for those who believe that they need some assistance. I've written it to help settle disputes between spouses, and between adult children and *their* parents or in-laws, over how children should be raised. I've written it both to reassure good parents that they are doing the right thing and to give parents who aren't very good the guidance they need to change.

If you read over the ten principles and say to yourself, "I already know this stuff," that's great. Read the book over from time to time to remind yourself to practice what you know. Use it when you need to reassure yourself that what you're doing is right, even when others tell you that you are wrong. And if you think you are already doing all the things I suggest, tell yourself to do them more often. I've never met a parent who is perfect 100 percent of the time. We all can improve our batting average.

What You Do Matters

Be a Mindful Parent
Genes Don't Make Parents Irrelevant
Children Learn by Watching
Handling Influences Outside the Family
Learn from Your Mistakes

Be a Mindful Parent

I'LL BET you've given a lot of thought to the way you want your child to turn out, but you've probably thought less about what you should be doing as a parent to actually help this happen.

You're certain, for instance, that you want your ten-year-old to do well in school, but perhaps you're not really sure what you should be doing to facilitate her scholastic success. Or maybe you want your toddler to be the sort of child who can play well with others, but you don't know how to make this happen. You want your child to be intellectually curious, but you have no idea what you should be doing as a parent to help stimulate his development in this direction.

This book contains a lot of information about different approaches to parenting and how your child is affected by them. In later sections, I'll be discussing the parenting strategies shown to contribute to school achievement, social competence, and intellectual inquisitiveness, as well as a wide array of other characteristics.

Before we get to those specifics, though, I want to draw a distinction between parenting that is mindful and parenting that is simply reactive and slapdash. By "mindful" parenting, I mean parenting that is intentional, where the consequences of your actions toward your child are the ones you've actually intended, rather than those that just happened by chance.

Strive to be a more mindful parent.

Saying that parenting should be intentional or mindful doesn't mean that it can't be spontaneous, or heartfelt, or natural. When I say that your parenting should be mindful, I don't mean that you should obsess over each and every decision you make, analyze to death every interaction you have with your child, or overthink yourself into parental paralysis. What I mean is that how you treat and respond to your child should come from a knowledgeable, deliberate sense of what you want to accomplish. Parenting can, and should, be heartfelt, and it often is impromptu, but it should never be haphazard or random. There should always be a method to your madness, even though you may not always be consciously aware of it.

Parents usually find themselves in one of three types of situations, and mindful parenting comes in handy in each one, although it does so in different ways.

The first type of situation is one where you have plenty of time to think through what you want to do before you act. This is when it is easiest to be mindful. You might be choosing among several preschools for your four-year-old and wondering which one is best, or trying to decide whether to force your junior high schooler to continue taking piano lessons, even though he has said that he wants to quit. You might be deliberating over whether your child is old enough to stay home without a babysitter in the evening, or whether your teenager is responsible enough to take a part-time job during the school year. You might be trying to decide how to respond to your child's request for a weekly allowance, or for permission to get her ears pierced or to use her savings to buy something special, expensive, and altogether unnecessary.

In all of these situations, you should take the opportunity to really think before you act. Always ask yourself this: What effect will my decision have on my child? If you parent mindfully—if you really *think* about what you want to accomplish before you act—you will be able to sort through the important issues, and you'll be better able to decide what's best for your child in the long run. Perhaps once you stop and think about it, you'll realize that the decision is actually easier than you think—or maybe you'll realize that it's far more complicated and requires more careful deliberation. Maybe you'll decide that talking it over with your spouse or another parent is a good idea. Whatever the outcome, you will have made an informed decision rather than an impulsive one.

The second type of situation parents often find themselves in is one where they need to react on the spot but nevertheless have a little time to think before responding. Your two-year-old has refused to eat what you've served her for dinner. Your six-year-old has just struck out for the third time in a row during his first Little League game. Your nine-year-old daughter calls you at work and asks if she and her friend can take a bus to the mall after school. Your teenager has come home from a party and told you that other kids at the party had been drinking. At these moments, you can't say to your child, "Can I get back to you about that tomorrow?" But you can pause and think before you respond.

In these sorts of situations, a mindful parent is able to resist the impulsive reaction ("Eat everything on your plate or you can't have dessert." "Don't be upset, sweetie, it's just a game." "No, you're too young to go without a parent." "You're not allowed to see those friends anymore."). If you parent mindfully, you can think through the situation and respond in a way that is consistent with the principles of effective parenting discussed in the rest of this book.

The third type of scenario is one where you might think that mindful parenting would be least useful, but where, in fact, just the opposite is true. This is the situation where you do not have time to think, where you have no choice but to respond reflexively.

Your toddler is throwing a temper tantrum in the frozen food aisle of the supermarket. Your seven-year-old is about to strangle her five-year-old brother. Your nine-year-old is so anxious about the first day of summer camp that he will not get dressed, even though the camp bus will arrive any minute. You get up in the middle of the night to get a glass of water and smell marijuana smoke wafting out of your teenager's bedroom. In these situations, a mindful parent responds instinctively, but her instincts are likely to be the right ones because she is familiar enough with the basic principles of good parenting and has employed them often enough under other, less pressing circumstances, that good parenting has become second nature.

In the same way that top athletes are able to perform well under pressure without thinking, parents who have really mastered the fundamentals of good parenting can parent effectively even when they don't have time to work through a reasoned response.

The more you make an effort to deliberately practice good parenting, the more instinctive it becomes. That's why it's especially important to develop good parenting habits when your child is young. It is always possible to acquire them when your child is older—it's never too late to improve—but parenting is sure easier if you start out with the right approach when you've just become a parent.

We are intentional and deliberate about so many of the things we do in life that it is hard to understand why anyone would be slapdash about something as important as parenting. You wouldn't think of running a business or overseeing an organization without being thoughtful about it. You don't (or you shouldn't) make decisions about your finances impulsively. We've all been told time and time again to think carefully and analyze our options before we make major purchases like homes, cars, or appliances. And yet, many people who are thoughtful business executives, superb financial planners, and astute consumers raise their children without really ever thinking about what they are doing.

I suppose that some people believe that parenting is one of those things that just comes naturally, or that thinking about it takes all the fun out of it. To tell you the truth, though, I've met very few "natural" parents. I've met parents who are thoughtful about what they do, however, and I've met those who parent by the seat of their pants, and, more often than not, the thoughtful parents have an awful lot more fun than the careless ones. It's hardly a surprise: When your parenting is thoughtful, your child is more likely to be better adjusted, and when your child is well-adjusted, it's considerably more fun to be a parent than when your child is having lots of problems and you're upset with how things are going.

Pay attention to how you parent. When you can, parent proactively rather than reactively. It's fine to be spontaneous, but try to be mindful.

Genes Don't Make Parents Irrelevant

IT SEEMS as though every other day we learn about some aspect of human nature that is linked to our genes. There is so much published about the extent to which our genes control who we are that it's easy to start wondering whether parents make any difference at all in how their children turn out. But there's a big difference between saying that genes matter (which is true) and saying that therefore parents don't make a difference (which is not true).

There is no question that children inherit tendencies to develop in certain directions. Some children are inclined to be more aggressive than others; some have a tendency to be more timid. Some children are genetically more likely to be extroverted; others are more likely to be introverted. But there is a big difference between saying that a child's character is *influenced* by his genes and saying that it is *determined* by them.

Let me give you an illustration of what I mean. We all know people who have a tendency to put on weight, and we know others who can eat and eat and never gain a pound. But this doesn't mean that the first type of person is destined to be obese and the second will inevitably be as thin as a pencil. All it means is that, to avoid becoming overweight, the first person has to eat a less fattening diet and exercise more vigorously than the second. By the same token, someone who is genetically predisposed toward shyness can learn to be outgoing, but it will take more work for that individual than it would for someone with a different genetic makeup.

This logic applies to raising children. The way a child is nurtured influences how his or her genetic nature is expressed. It would certainly be difficult (but not impossible) to take a child with an inherited tendency to be timid and make that child aggressive, or vice versa. But whether a child who is predisposed to be aggressive develops into a playground bully or well-behaved hockey player will be determined by how the child is raised, not by his genes. The environment will determine whether a child's genetic tendency toward being inhibited will be manifested in his being painfully withdrawn or simply more reserved than other children. Children who are genetically predisposed to be aggressive just need extra help from their parents in learning how to control their aggression, and children who are inclined to be timid just need extra encouragement to overcome their shyness. In other

words, the ultimate manifestation of your child's genetic temperament depends on how your child is raised, and not simply on his
or her DNA.

Regardless of your child's genetic makeup, what you do as a
parent matters tremendously, because it is your influence that affects how those genes are expressed. We know that genes influence children's intelligence, for example, but we also know that all
children profit from having their parents read to them regularly.

You have the ability to influence your child's personality, interests, character, intelligence, attitudes, and values. You can influence your child's likes and dislikes. You can influence how your
child behaves at home, at school, and with friends. You can influence whether your child is kind and considerate or mean and
selfish.

There isn't a more important influence on your child's development than you, including your child's genes.

What you do matters.

Tell yourself that every day.

Children Learn by Watching

HAVE YOU EVER looked in the mirror and seen one of your parents' facial expressions in your own reflection? Have you ever
heard yourself say something to your child that your parents said
to you when you were growing up? Have you ever noticed that
you have many of the same attitudes, opinions, and habits that
your parents had when you were growing up, even though you
swore you would grow up to be different?

Now that you're a parent, the tables have turned. Your child is
acquiring your expressions, your opinions, and your habits from
you just as you did from your own parents. And in many
instances, neither you nor your child is even aware of it when it is
happening. You are on stage all the time, and your child is in the
audience, right there in the front row of the orchestra section.

Children enter the world primed to model their parents' behavior. There is nothing that parents can do to prevent this. The capacity for children to imitate their parents is so strong that scientists now think it is part of our evolved history as human beings. If you take a baby who is barely a few days old, for example, hold her so that she can focus on your face, and then stick your tongue out at her, she will move her tongue back at you. (She may not yet have the muscle control to stick her tongue out in exactly the same way that you do, but if you look closely, you will see that she does move her tongue in response to you moving yours.) Imitating adults, especially parents, is a natural part of who we are. In fact, children's ability to learn by watching is present long before their ability to learn from others' attempts to deliberately teach them.

Watching parents is more than "monkey-see, monkey-do," though. One way that children learn about the world is by making sense of the behavior of the adults around them. Even before they can talk, for example, babies monitor their parents for signals about whether they are safe or in danger. When your infant is approached by a stranger—for instance, when you and your seven-month-old are out in public and someone comes over to tell you how pretty your child is—the baby will usually look at you before "deciding" whether to worry or fret. If you look anxious and nervous, your child will be more likely to cry or be fearful when the stranger approaches than if you look happy and welcoming. Similarly, when crawling about the room, a six-month-old will often pause and glance over his shoulder, waiting for a signal from Mom before continuing on in his travels. He's not just making sure that Mom is still in the room; he's trying to read Mom's expression to see if what he's about to do is safe.

When your child is exploring her world, what signals are you sending?

Parents are not always aware of the subtle messages they

communicate to their children through their actions and emotions. If your preschooler is climbing a tree, a frightened look on
your face tells him not only that you are afraid, but that the situation is something for *him* to be afraid of. If you were to stand
under the same tree with a big smile on your face, your child
would infer something entirely different. This is one reason
anxious parents often produce anxious children. It's not just
that anxiety is inherited (it is, in part); it's also that anxiety is
contagious, and children are especially susceptible to the emotions that their parents transmit.

As children get older, they watch their parents for guidance in
a wide range of situations, not just to distinguish between what is
safe and what isn't. If your child sees you and your spouse consistently resolving disputes by screaming and yelling, for example, or
through physical fighting, your child will come to believe that the
best way to settle disagreements with another person is to slug it
out. If you and your spouse rarely raise your voice to each other,
though, your child is unlikely to resort to this sort of tactic when
interacting with others. Parents who tell their child not to hit but
who themselves are physically aggressive may be surprised to find
that their children imitate this in their own subsequent relationships with friends, dates, and members of their family. This is one
reason that children who have been physically abused are more
likely than others to grow up to be violent in their marriage or
abusive toward their own children.

Children are also inclined to model their parents' behavior
because they have a strong, almost inborn, desire to grow up to be
just like their mother or father. You can see just how strong the
tendency for children to imitate their parents is when you eaves-
drop on your child's play. When their son or daughter is playing
with another child, it's not uncommon for parents to overhear
their own words coming out of their child's mouth. (When those
words are witty or wise, you smile and feel proud, but when those

words are laced with profanity, it's a different matter altogether.)
A child who punishes her dolls by putting them on a time-out,
withholding love, or spanking them has probably received this
sort of discipline herself. A child who reads to her stuffed animals
in a calm and soothing voice has probably been soothed in this
exact way, or maybe has seen a brother or sister being read to in
this manner. When children play at being a parent, they are often
mimicking the parenting they themselves have received or witnessed.

Most parents underestimate the degree to which their children
are aware of what they do and say. I think we get so used to our
children *not* paying attention to us when we want them to mind
us that we forget how closely they are listening to us when we'd
rather they didn't. But children have an extraordinary talent for
appearing to be lost in their own thoughts when they are actually
paying very close attention. You and your spouse might think that
your child, deeply engrossed in her coloring book, is not even
aware that you are discussing your family's precarious finances,
but she is almost sure to be taking everything in, even if some of it
is beyond her full understanding. And if there is anxiety or tension in your conversation, she will certainly pick up on it.

And don't think that you are being observed by your children
only when you are at home. Your child watches and learns from
your behavior outside the house as well. You're being observed by
your child when you are waiting in the checkout line in the grocery store, ordering food in a restaurant, talking with fellow parents on the playground, or chatting with other passengers in the
airport. If you are courteous, kind, and friendly, chances are your
child will turn out similarly. If you are rude, nasty, or standoffish,
your child will learn that this is the appropriate way to act toward
others. Your child learns how to interact with other people by
watching you.

Learning by observing continues throughout childhood and
adolescence, too, although as they get older, children are less apt

to imitate their parents explicitly and more likely to mimic them in more subtle ways. Even though it seems as if you are the last thing on your older child's mind, your preadolescent or teenager is all too aware of how you spend your free time, how you balance work and family life, how you have fun, and how you cope with stress. Teenagers especially enjoy noting the difference between what their parents say and what they actually do. If your child sees that you cope with problems by using or abusing alcohol, for example, your lectures on the dangers of drinking will have little impact on your teenager's behavior.

This does not mean that children invariably turn out to be carbon copies of their parents. After all, although you are the most important role model for your child, you are not the only one; children learn from other family members, from their peers, and from things they see on television. But they watch their parents more closely than anyone else. This is especially true prior to adolescence.

You may think it's fine to scream at your spouse, sprinkle your speech with profanities, make bigoted comments, brag about cheating on your taxes, or drink more beer than you should from time to time. But please, don't do these things in front of your child.

You may have your share of irrational fears and anxieties, but there is no earthly reason why you need to model these for your son or daughter.

Parents have always said to their children, "Do as I say, not as I do," but children never heed this advice. Children learn more by observing their parents than they do by listening to their lectures. That's why you need to be careful about what you say and what you do when your child can hear or see you.

You can't choose when or whether to be your child's role model. Whether you like it or not, your child is always learning by watching you.

Handling Influences Outside the Family

THE FACT that you are the most important influence on your child does not mean that you are the *only* influence. Your child's classmates, friends, and favorite cartoon shows all have the potential to affect his behavior.

What's a parent to do in light of the wide range of influences that children are exposed to outside the family?

Let me answer this question by first saying what you should *not* do.

Don't shrug your shoulders and lament that you are powerless in the face of these other forces. This simply is not true.

Don't point your finger at your child's best friend, boyfriend, or girlfriend and say that he or she is entirely responsible for your child's undesirable behavior. Children choose their friends, and parents influence the choices their children make.

Don't blame your child's behavior on the television networks, the latest music, or the Internet. If you object to what your child looks at, listens to, or surfs through, there are plenty of ways to exert your influence.

There is no question that peer groups and the mass media play a greater role in the upbringing of today's children than they had in past generations. With more and more parents working full time, children spend less time with adults and more time with age-mates and plugged into electronic media than their parents did when they were growing up. The array of media choices available to today's youngsters is staggering: hundreds of free, cable, and premium television channels; freestanding, handheld, and Web-based video games; first-run and prerecorded films; music on the radio, on CD or tape, and delivered over the Internet; thousands of paper and electronic magazines; and literally millions of uncensored chat rooms and Web sites. And almost all of this is available twenty-four hours a day, seven days a week.

Moreover, much of the time children spend plugged in or with their friends is either completely unsupervised or only modestly so. The vast majority of American schoolchildren have a television in their bedroom, where they can watch what they want, when they want to. Millions of schoolchildren spend the after-school hours without an adult in sight.

Given these conditions, it's easy to understand why parents often look anywhere but at themselves to explain their children's problems. What could be more convenient than saying that your child's excessive aggression is caused by playing too many video games, or that her drug use is due to the corrupting influence of her boyfriend?

The truth of the matter is that although children *are* influenced by the friends they spend time with and the television they watch, their friends and media preferences are choices, and parents can influence and constrain the choices they make. Children don't pick their friends haphazardly, nor do they randomly choose what they view, listen to, or amuse themselves with. Their decisions are influenced by you.

I've already told you what you *shouldn't* do. Now, here's what you *should* do.

Understand that one of the ways you make a difference as a parent is through your role as the "manager" of your child's leisure and time with friends. If you don't want to be overshadowed by these outside influences, don't leave these activities completely up to your child's discretion.

When your child is young, you can manage his friendships by steering him toward peers you want him to play with and away from ones you don't. He will see children at school whom you don't especially care for, of course, but you have control over the children he sees after school and on weekends. Over time, your choice of play-date partners will send a message to him about your likes and dislikes. Don't be shy about saying nice things about children who you think are positive influences ("I really like Julie—she's such a friendly person," or "I'm so happy you're starting to be friends with Michael—he seems like he's a lot of fun to play with"). Although it's never too late to try to influence your child's choice of friends, it is much easier if you begin early.

When your child is in elementary school, get her involved in activities that are likely to bring her into contact with children who will be good influences, those who share healthy interests in school, athletics, or the arts. It is all well and good to provide private lessons in music, dance, or sports, but remember that after school is also a time for helping to get your child into positive peer groups. Make sure you know who your child's friends are. (If you are not sure, ask at your next school conference. Teachers can be a very good source of information about this.) And keep up the talk about which friends you admire and which ones you don't. The main thing to remember, though, is that you can influence your child's *friends* by influencing your child's *interests*. This indirect approach often works better than a more direct attempt to regulate whom she can and cannot be friends with.

It's important to be firm about how your child spends her free time at this age, because this will have a major effect on her choice of friends. If she is involved in an extracurricular activity she feels passionate about—it doesn't matter whether it is athletic, artistic, musical, or service-oriented—she's far less likely to end up associating with friends who will lead her down the wrong road.

When your child is a teenager, continue to influence his friends by influencing his interests. In addition, get to know his friends, and don't be shy about speaking candidly about those you like and the ones you are less fond of. Be sure to give a reason and have some evidence to back it up ("I wish you wouldn't hang around with Susan—she always seems to be getting into trouble at school"). Don't expect your teenager to drop a relationship just because you've expressed an occasional negative opinion. But if you are consistent* with your message, it will gradually sink in. During adolescence this takes a fair amount of time, so it is best to start early if you can. And, of course, don't let your child spend time with kids who are genuinely dangerous.

You should also manage your child's media usage. The media are less of an influence over your child's development than either you or your child's friends, but children are nevertheless affected by the television shows, videos, and films to which they are exposed, especially as far as violence is concerned. Children who see a lot of aggressive content or who play a lot of violent video games are more likely to behave aggressively. (The evidence concerning the effects of violence in music is not so clear-cut.) And remember that the amount of time spent watching or playing matters: The more exposure, the more aggression.

There is no reason you cannot put a limit on the amount and content of your child's television and video-game usage. If you put a television in your child's bedroom, have no rules about what he is permitted to watch, and don't regulate how much time he can watch, you have no right to complain about the evil influence of television on your child's development and behavior. If your child has her own computer, you can easily equip it with filters to block highly sexual or violent content.

The key to understanding how you can maintain your authority in the face of powerful forces outside your home is understanding the role you play in shaping your child's choices of friends and activities. Rather than telling yourself that you are powerless against these overwhelming influences, you should tell yourself that their very power is what makes your involvement so crucial. The strength of peer influence and the pervasiveness of the mass media don't make parents irrelevant. It's just the opposite: Their existence makes parents more important today than ever.

Are you are concerned about the potential negative influence of peers or the media on your child? If so, don't throw up your hands in despair or shirk your responsibility. Assert your authority as a parent—that's what parents are for.

Learn from Your Mistakes

WE ALL make mistakes as parents. We're short with our kids when we're tired or stressed out. We forget to ask about things that are going on at school when we're preoccupied with our own work. We occasionally act too leniently because we're too exhausted to enforce the rules we've made, or we act too severely simply because we're in a bad mood. No one is a model parent all the time.

When you've made a mistake as a parent, don't beat yourself up over it. Your child will not be permanently scarred because you lost your temper, forgot to praise a project for school, argued nastily with your spouse within your child's earshot, or missed an important soccer match. Children are much more affected by the enduring conditions of their home environment than by isolated events, even when those events are dramatic ones. What matters is the overall climate your child is exposed to over time. Children are rarely influenced by single decisions or incidents, unless the event was absolutely traumatic. And even in the face of trauma, children are remarkably resilient.

This is why it's so important to understand your mistakes as a parent and to learn from them. When you understand why you made a mistake, you can figure out what went wrong and take steps to minimize the chances of it happening again, so that this sort of errant parenting doesn't become a regular part of your child's home environment.

The circumstances that get in the way of good parenting differ from parent to parent, so a little self-analysis is necessary for you to figure out your own vulnerabilities. Some parents find that they are at their worst when they are rushed—that this tends to make them short-tempered or inattentive. If you find that you make mistakes in these situations—that this is when you are likely to say or do something you later regret—learn to avoid making important parenting decisions when things around the house are frenetic. If your child asks your permission for something important when you are rushing around trying to get ready for work, for instance, learn that the best response at the time is "I'd like to think about it a bit—let's talk about it later." If your child presses you for an immediate response, don't give in unless it is absolutely necessary (for example, if she is asking permission to go on a field trip at school that is scheduled for that very day). But if this happens frequently, explain to your child that the morning "rush hour" is not the best time to have this sort of conversation. Make it a habit of checking in with your child about this sort of thing the night before.

The same goes for parents who don't parent well when they are preoccupied with other things. You might have an important deadline to meet at work, or be going through a rough time with your spouse, or be thinking about a relative or friend who is ill. Some people are able to "compartmentalize" better than others; they can set aside these sorts of concerns and pay full attention to their child when need be. But other parents—maybe you're one of them—have a tougher time preventing demands from one aspect of life from interfering with their responsibilities as a parent. If this spillover is a problem for you, be aware when you are distracted by other things, and force yourself to devote your complete attention to parenting when you have to. Sometimes just knowing that we are preoccupied with something is all we need to be able to put that issue aside temporarily.

Other parents are fine under the pressure of time or when they are preoccupied, but perform poorly when they are tired. If this describes you, you should take this into account when you've just walked in the door after a long day at the office, a mind-numbing commute, or a fitful night's sleep. There's nothing wrong with telling your child that you want to hear all about school after you've had a little time to freshen up and revive yourself. That's better than pretending to listen when you're not really paying attention.

You should also remember that good parenting is very hard to do when you're angry or upset. When you are angry with your child or upset for some other reason, your emotions can easily spill over into your parenting. We can't help feeling angry or upset with our children from time to time, but, as a rule, it's not a good idea to discipline children when you're mad or distressed. Your anger may be perfectly legitimate (for instance, your child borrowed something valuable or irreplaceable without asking you and has broken it), but you'll exercise better judgment as a parent if you calm down and wait for your anger to subside a bit. It's fine to come right out and say to your child, "I'm too angry to talk about this right now. Let's wait until we can talk about this calmly." Believe me, your child will thank you for it.

If you've made a mistake as a parent, there is no point in pretending that what you did was right. It's important for parents to admit their mistakes, to their spouse and to their child, as long as they do so in a way that the child can understand. If you say to your child, "I'm sorry that I snapped at you before. I had a bad day at work and I took it out on you," or, "I've thought about the discussion we had last night, and I think you were probably right," your child will not think less of you. In fact, just the opposite is likely to happen: When children see that their parents are willing to admit their mistakes, they are much more likely to respect their parents' point of view in the future because they know the parent has respect for their opinion. This is also one of the best ways to teach your child that the right thing to do when you've wronged somebody else is to apologize.

I've said that reading this book will help you become a better parent. I didn't say that it would turn you into a perfect parent. There's no such thing as a perfect parent. When you've overreacted, underreacted, or reacted incorrectly, admit that you were wrong, strive to do a little better the next time, and move on.

You Cannot Be Too Loving

Can You Spoil Your Child with Love?

Expressing Physical Affection

Praise Your Child's Accomplishments

Responding to Your Child's Emotional Needs

Providing a Safe Haven

Can You Spoil Your Child with Love?

IF PARENTS would worry more about not paying enough attention to their children and less about spoiling them, the world would be a better place.

I can think of plenty of children who have suffered because their parents were too busy, too selfish, or too preoccupied to attend to their needs. But I've never met a child who was worse off because his parents loved him too much. It is simply not possible to spoil a child with love.

What we often think of as the product of spoiling a child is never the result of showing a child too much love. It is usually the consequence of giving a child things *in place of* love—things like leniency, lowered expectations, or material possessions. Children are harmed when their parents don't set limits for them, when parents lower their expectations for them as a way of being nice, or when toys or food or gifts are used to substitute for genuine affection or attention.

When it comes to genuine expressions of warmth and affection, you cannot love your child too much.

What does this mean, in concrete terms?

Your child will not be harmed by being told every single day that you love him. Your child will not be harmed by being reminded that she is a source of endless happiness for you. Your child will not be hurt by being showered with physical affection, with care, and with praise when it's heartfelt and well deserved. Don't hold back your affection or act aloof because you think your child will become spoiled by all the attention.

Many years ago it was believed that holding back love would help develop a child's character. Perhaps there is someone in your life now who believes in the "old school" of raising children, who has cautioned you against being too loving toward your child.

That old school of thought has turned out to be wrong. In literally thousands of studies, psychologists have looked at the connection between how much love parents show their children and their children's adjustment. If it were possible to spoil children by loving them too much—if the old school were correct—you would expect these studies to find that the best-adjusted children come from homes where parents are somewhat distant or hold back a bit on their expression of love. But I can't think of a single study that has ever found this. In study after study of parent-child relationships, the best-adjusted children always report the highest levels of parental love.

There are still some parents who believe in the old school of child rearing. Some think that children need to be toughened, and that too much love will make a child fragile. (This is the "school of hard knocks" approach to parenting.) Some think that children who get a lot of parental affection will grow up to be weak. (You hear this sometimes from fathers who worry that too much love will interfere with their son's masculinity.) Other parents believe that parental affection, praise, or concern will somehow make their child needy and that their child will have abnormally high requirements for attention or care when they get older. They are convinced that by withholding love, they somehow will raise a child whose need for being loved is lower.

In fact, just the opposite is true. When children feel genuinely loved, they develop such a strong sense of security that they almost always are less needy. As a result, the emotionally neediest adults are typically those who did not receive sufficient parental love while growing up, or whose parents' love was either inconsistent or less than genuine. The healthiest adults, and the ones who themselves are able to express their love to others, are invariably those who grew up feeling unequivocally and unconditionally loved by their parents, not those who were forced to scrape by on something less than complete affection.

A famous study of whether parents should respond to their baby's cries during the middle of the night made this point very nicely. Contrary to those who believe that comforting a baby who cries out will only reward the baby's behavior and lead to more crying, the researchers found that the opposite is true. Babies who are comforted when they cry out during the night tend to cry less, not more, over time. The reason is simple enough: Babies cry out when they wake during the night because they are scared and disoriented. Being comforted makes them feel more secure, and this enables them to sleep better.

The surest way to keep a baby crying out every night is to ignore the baby's emotional needs. And the surest way to raise an emotionally needy child is to withhold your love and affection.

Don't confuse *whether* you show your child affection with *how* you do it. Showering your child with physical affection, compliments, praise, attention, and verbal affirmations of how much you enjoy spending time together are all good—and the more often, the better. If you want to buy your child fancy presents, take him on expensive outings, treat him to his favorite foods, or grant him special privileges, these things are fine, too, so long as they are done in moderation and so long as you don't use them to substitute for genuine expressions of love. (If you do, you won't be fooling anyone but yourself. Children know the difference between being truly loved and being bought off.)

One of my mentors, the brilliant child psychologist Urie Bronfenbrenner, once said that every child needs at least one adult who is "irrationally committed" to the child. It's this emotional bond that allows children to grow up to be psychologically healthy.

Don't be afraid to show your "irrational commitment" to your son or daughter. When it comes to genuinely expressing your love for your child, you can't overdo it.

Expressing Physical Affection

CHILDREN NEED PLENTY of physical affection from their parents, not just when they are infants, but throughout childhood and adolescence. We humans are tactile creatures, and we have a natural need for physical contact with others.

Sometimes it seems that parents have become so concerned with their children's intellectual development that they overlook the child's more basic needs, such as the need to be touched. We spend so much time worrying about what we can do to make our children smarter that we often forget that the foundation of a good relationship between parent and child is emotional and physical, not intellectual. All those educational toys that promise to stimulate your child's learning might make you feel like you're being a good parent, but in the long run they hardly make a difference in your child's development. Your toddler will benefit much more from rolling around on the floor with you than from a fancy mobile over her crib or a session with flash cards designed to teach her a foreign language or the multiplication tables.

The benefits of physical contact between parent and child are more than just psychological. It's not simply that it feels nice to your child to be held close to you. Infants in many species—not just humans, but other mammals as well—develop in healthier ways when they are gently and affectionately touched by their parents. Touching stimulates physical growth, reduces stress, and helps the immune system function better. And, by the way, if you *are* one of those parents who can't stop thinking about what you should be doing to make your child smarter, you'll find it comforting to know that new studies show that physical contact between parents and their babies even stimulates the child's brain development. Wrestling with your toddler won't guarantee his later admission to an Ivy League school, but it will likely help foster his intellectual growth, and it won't cost you a dime.

The benefits of physical affection between you and your child are not just for your child, though. Your own emotional attachment to your child will be strengthened by regular physical contact. In other words, taking the time to rock your child to sleep before putting her to bed is as good for you as it is for her. This is especially important for fathers to keep in mind, because they are less apt than mothers to have passing physical contact with their child as part of ordinary child-rearing activities such as feeding, dressing, and bathing. This is also important for parents who work long hours and who rely a lot on other child-care providers. You need to remind yourself from time to time that physical contact with your child is crucial to the healthy development of your relationship.

Most parents find it easy to express physical affection when their child is a baby, because so much moment-to-moment child rearing during infancy has a physical component. It's not hard to stroke your child's face while nursing him or giving him a bottle, kiss him while you're putting him into his car seat, rub his back while you're sharing a picture book, play with his toes while giving him a bath, or tickle him while you're getting him dressed. Even as a toddler, your child gives you plenty of opportunities to hug, hold, and kiss him.

As your child moves into the preschool years, though, you have to make a more conscious and deliberate effort to express your affection physically as well as verbally. You have fewer natural opportunities to hug and kiss your child now that she is three or four, because she is now able to dress herself, feed herself, and move about the house without you carrying her. But just because your child is now more physically capable and verbally fluent doesn't mean that she needs your physical affection any less. You just have to create your own opportunities.

Be mindful of the fact that your child may resist some of your efforts to be physically affectionate if they make him feel as if he is still a little baby. Once they are four or five years old, very few children like being ordered to kiss on command or enjoy being smothered while being told that they are someone's darling little baby. *You* may wish your preschooler were still a newborn, but this is the last thing he has on *his* mind.

This is why your child holds your hand absentmindedly while watching a cartoon with you but resists holding your hand when ordered to do so in public. It's not that he doesn't like being touched by you—he does. He just doesn't want to be touched in a way that undermines his feelings of being grown up. (This doesn't mean that you shouldn't make your child hold your hand when safety considerations require it: when you are crossing the street, for instance, or walking through a crowded department store. It's just not an expression of affection under these circumstances.)

Parents don't always realize that children need physical affection even after they have reached a stage where they may seem too grown up for overt displays of it. Sometimes you just have to be a little subtle in when and how you express it. There is no reason to make a big deal about it; in fact, expressing your affection for your child physically probably is more satisfying for your child when it is a natural, day-to-day part of your relationship. In other words, learn to express physical affection toward your child without announcing that you are doing it or making a big show of it—with a quick kiss before she leaves for school in the morning, a hug when she returns in the afternoon, a shoulder rub when she is leaning over the kitchen table doing her homework, or a back massage while you tuck her in for the night. All of this physical contact, however subtle and low-key, reinforces and strengthens your emotional connection to each other. Many parents find this hard to do, but it's very important that you try. Over time, it will become easier.

While children are trying to develop a sense of independence during preschool and early elementary school, they often will balk at shows of physical affection that take place in public. Your five-going-on-sixteen-year-old does not want the world to know that he is still someone's little boy. So be aware of the difference between being physically affectionate when you and your child are alone (or when no one outside the immediate family is around) versus when others are able to see, and don't take it personally if your child doesn't seem to enjoy public displays of affection. If you are buckling your child into the backseat of your car, for example, it may be just fine to give him a hug and a kiss when it's just the two of you, but he probably will find the same behavior intrusive and embarrassing if his best friend is sitting next to him. It doesn't mean that your child wants you to stop hugging or kissing him; he just wants you to stop doing it when his friends can see. (Of course, even when a friend is sitting next to your child, you can always give your child a special smile and a secret squeeze.)

Embarrassment over public displays of parental affection generally reaches its peak during early adolescence, but this embarrassment should not be taken as an indicator of emotional distance on the part of the child. Many parents find that their young teenager will not permit them so much as a hug if it can be witnessed by someone else, and the witness doesn't even have to be a classmate or friend. Again, this has nothing to do with your adolescent's feelings toward you, either as a person or as a parent. Your teenager is busy letting the world know that she is an adult (at least, that's what she hopes the world sees when she is on view), and she'd just as soon keep the fact that she even *has* parents a secret.

When you pick your son or daughter up from school, a quick hug might be all you are permitted—if even that. But the same adolescent may be perfectly fine with a greater display of affection when you are home alone. I know plenty of teenagers who shun their parents' physical contact in public but enjoy it at home, and there is no good reason why you can't respect your adolescent's wishes to keep this part of your relationship private, at least during this stage of his development. As long as you don't make a federal case of it, this situation almost always eases up once your child has passed through middle adolescence. Once they are confident that the world sees them as young adults, teenagers usually relax and let their parents go back to expressing physical affection in public.

Some parents hold back on physical affection once their child becomes a teenager because they are uncomfortable with their child's developing sexuality. This is often a special concern for fathers of daughters and mothers of sons. There is no reason for this, however. You know the difference between physical affection that is sexual and physical affection that is not, and so does your child. Hugging or kissing your teenager in a nonsexual way is not only fine, it is beneficial to your teenager's development. During a time when their body is changing so dramatically and unpredictably, it is reassuring to adolescents to feel the hug of someone whose touch is familiar and comforting. Your teenager won't tell you this, but it is likely to be true.

You can't be too affectionate toward your child. Just be sensitive to the way your child wants you to express yourself.

Praise Your Child's Accomplishments

WHEN YOUR CHILD has mastered something difficult, let her know that you admire what she's done. The achievement can be as rudimentary as pulling herself up to a standing position in her crib, or it can be as sophisticated as mastering a complex piece of music for the violin. It can be figuring out how to sound out a word when your child is first learning how to read, or it can be finishing up a semester-long paper or science project. Take time to stand back and marvel at what your child has just done, and then let him know how impressed you are. You seldom see children as proud as when they've been told by a parent that they've done something really well—and you seldom see children as upset when their parents have failed to notice their achievements.

Praising children not only makes them feel good about themselves, though; it helps them learn important lessons about the value of working hard to achieve a goal. All children should experience the feeling of satisfaction that comes from succeeding when you've tried hard to accomplish something, and the origins of this feeling are largely in the "oohs" and "aahs" they receive from their parents.

Some parents worry that praising children too often makes them feel as if their parents' love is conditional—that their worth is entirely wrapped up in what they do, rather than who they are. I suppose that if the only kind words you ever said to your child were linked to his or her accomplishments this might happen. But this will not be a problem if you express your love and affection at all sorts of different times, and not simply when your child has accomplished or succeeded at something.

The *way* you praise your child is important, though, so you need to be careful about a few things. In other words, think about how you phrase your praise.

First, *try to phrase your reactions in ways that praise the specific accomplishment,* rather than link the accomplishment to your affection for your child. Saying "You did a great job on your book report" is better than saying "I love it when you do so well at school." The first remark contains praise for the book report, not a judgment about the child's worth. The latter remark conveys the message that your love is contingent on your child's academic performance. (Even if you don't mean it this way, if your child hears this sort of thing often enough, she will start to feel that this is true.) You can both love your child and have high expectations, but one should have nothing to do with the other, either in your mind or in your child's.

Second, *focus your praise on the link between the accomplishment and the effort your child exerted,* rather than attributing your child's achievement to some "natural" or innate characteristic. Telling your child that her piano recital was a big success because she put so much work into preparing for it sends a very different message than telling her that her performance was a success because she is a naturally gifted musician. The first statement reinforces the idea that hard work pays off; the second suggests that individuals' accomplishments are mainly a function of their natural talents. Believing that how well you perform is due to your innate abilities is all well and good when you succeed, but it's a big problem when you don't. When your child doesn't do well at something, you want her to tell herself that the next time she needs to practice more or prepare more, rather than thinking "Well, I'm just no good at that."

Conveying the idea that people's accomplishments are determined by their inborn abilities is especially problematic when it comes to school achievement. All too often we tell our children that some people are just naturally gifted at certain subjects, or worse, that your ability to excel at something depends on your gender ("You're a girl—of course you have trouble with computers!"). Children so often hear from their parents that some people are naturally good at certain subjects, like math or foreign languages, that they start to believe that if they haven't succeeded on the first try, they simply must not have what it takes. This belief only makes them try less hard in the future because they are convinced that exerting effort is pointless. Parents should be especially careful about conveying these unintentional messages when their children first start receiving grades and are trying to make sense out of what they mean.

I know that children have natural strengths and weaknesses that affect their accomplishments in and out of school, but even the most gifted individuals in any field work hard to perform well. Michael Jordan, probably the best natural basketball player in the history of the game, is also legendary for the amount of time he spent practicing long after his teammates had quit for the day. As an adult, you've had time to learn that successful people in any field almost always work harder and practice more than their peers, regardless of how "naturally" talented they are. Your child has not yet learned this, though, and it's important that he does. Children are not innately gifted at everything they are asked to do, and your child needs to understand that success at anything is linked to how much effort you expend. So when you praise your child's accomplishments, be sure to draw attention to his or her hard work.

Third, *tie your praise to the quality of the accomplishment, not to the grade or rating it has received from someone else.* Saying "I'm really proud of how well you spell" is far better than saying "I'm really proud of the A you got on your spelling test." By the time your child is eight or nine, he already is painfully aware that his accomplishments are being graded and evaluated by others. He doesn't need you to point this out, too.

Fourth, I think that children's accomplishments ought to stand on their own, but *if you feel you must compare your child's performance to something, compare it to her previous level of accomplishment and not to the accomplishments of others.* "You've never hit the ball better" is a much better way to compliment your child's tennis playing than "You hit the ball so much better than the other kids."

Competition among children in the classroom and the playing field is fierce enough without your adding to it.

Finally, a word about emphasizing to your child that "he tried his best." I think this is a valuable sentiment to express when children are younger, but this reaction becomes less useful as children get older. By the time children have reached third grade or so, they know full well that people are judged mainly by their accomplishments and only marginally by their efforts. (We might not like this, but there's no denying that it's true.) When you tell your twelve-year-old that it doesn't matter how well he played in a soccer game or how he did on his science test as long as he tried his best, he knows that you're not being completely honest. If your child is disappointed in his performance, it's probably more helpful to try to figure out how to improve it next time than to fill the air with empty clichés.

The same holds true when it comes to false praise. When your child has performed poorly, don't criticize her (she feels bad enough without you rubbing it in), but don't lie and tell her she's done well, either. She knows when she hasn't, and praising her when it is unwarranted just diminishes the value of praise when it is genuinely deserved. Instead, focus on how she might do better the next time.

Just because your child enjoys your praise doesn't mean that this is the only thing that is motivating him. It simply feels good to know that the people you care about are excited that you've excelled at something.

Responding to Your Child's Emotional Needs

BEING A good parent involves so many different things. It must have one of the longest job descriptions ever created.

Parents take care of their children's physical needs, making sure that they are fed, bathed, clothed, and protected from illness and injury. They provide guidance and direction by setting limits, sharing wisdom, imparting values, and offering counsel and advice. Parents instruct, both by being teachers and by being role models. They help their children navigate the world outside the home by managing their relationships with peers and adults outside the family. They advocate for their children outside the home, making sure that their children are treated fairly by their teachers, their coaches, and other adults with whom they come into contact.

All of these functions are important. But maybe the most important thing that parents do is respond to their child's emotional needs. By this, I don't simply mean comforting your child when he's crying or reassuring her when she's afraid. Responding to your child's emotional needs also entails reacting in ways that helps your child's emotional development.

Your child needs to be able to draw emotional fuel from you in order to grow up psychologically healthy and happy. This role is a dual-edged sword for you as a parent. On the one hand, it feels wonderful to be depended on. But at the same time, this dependence can be incredibly draining. And unlike other relationships in your life, where you can say to the other person, "I really can't be depended on right now—I'm just too spent," as a parent you seldom have the freedom to be able to say this. (Single parents have it especially rough in this department. At least married parents can ask their spouse to spell them once in a while.)

Part of the reason that responding to your child's emotional needs can be so draining is that you often have to invest a fair amount of energy just figuring out what his needs are. When your child is broadcasting his emotions—when he's crying after falling down or trembling after a nightmare—it's pretty easy to guess what he needs from you. But when you are not sure just what you should do, understanding how your child's emotional needs change as he matures will enable you to understand how best to respond. In other words, the key to being an emotionally responsive parent is understanding your child's emotional development.

For each stage of development, there is always a central question that you should ask yourself. If you understand the specific question that is relevant to each period and why it arises when it does, you'll be better able to figure out what your child needs from you. The specific things you do will vary from situation to situation. But here are the general developmental guidelines you should keep in mind:

Infancy. When your child is a baby, his emotional needs revolve around developing a sense of security. Your baby needs to feel that the world is a safe place and that the surprises it holds in store for him are happy ones. You can make him feel this way by being calm, soothing, predictable, and affectionate. When your child is an infant and you're not sure what to do, ask yourself this: *How can I help my child feel more secure?*

Toddlerhood. When your child moves from infancy into toddlerhood, her emotional concerns shift from security to independence. She is developing a sense of herself as a separate person who can make her own decisions. She knows what she wants—or at least she thinks she does—and she doesn't want you or anyone else to get in the way. Your toddler needs to feel as if she is in charge. Your role is to help your child feel in charge without actually giving up your authority as a parent. If you're not sure how to respond to your toddler's needs, ask yourself this: *How can I help my child feel more in control?*

Early childhood. During early childhood, children are beginning to learn about the world outside of home and starting to envision themselves as grown-up participants in the larger society. Despite these daydreams and fantasies, though, preschoolers feel small and powerless, and they know that there is a huge gap between what they want and what they are capable of. As I once heard a frustrated five-year-old complain to his father as he was trying to peer over a crowd of adults blocking his view, "The world was built for grown-ups." Your role is to help your preschooler feel that his dream of becoming a grown-up is an achievable one. When your child is between four and six, ask yourself this: *What can I do to help my child feel more grown up?*

Elementary school. As your child moves into and through elementary school, she is expected to learn a huge assortment of things—not just academic skills, but extracurricular and social skills as well. She's trying to figure out how to be a good student, how to be popular with other kids, how to do everything from reading musical notes, to riding a skateboard, to helping bathe the family dog. And she knows that people—her teachers, her classmates, her friends, and her parents—are frequently evaluating her performance. What does she need at this point? She needs to feel competent. Your role is to help her identify what she's good at and to become better at the things she needs and wants to master. When your child is this age, you should be asking yourself this: *How can I help my child feel more capable?*

Early adolescence. When your child becomes an adolescent, around age twelve or so, his emotional needs change yet again. In many ways, the emotional needs of your twelve- or thirteen-year-old parallel those that were central when he was a toddler, when independence was on his mind. But your adolescent's needs are different in important respects. He wants to be independent, but in a way that is much more psychological than before. He needs to become an intellectually and emotionally separate person from you, one with his own beliefs, values, and opinions. Your role is to help him become more of an individual without severing your relationship with him. (Ironic though it may be, although the whole point of emotional development at this point is for your teenager to not feel dependent on you, you play a huge role in helping this independence to develop.) When your child has entered adolescence, your question for yourself is this: *How can I help my teenager feel more independent?*

Late adolescence. Once they have turned fifteen or sixteen, adolescents start to think more deeply about who they are and where they are headed. In many of the same ways that the emotional needs of toddlers (feeling in charge) give rise to the emotional needs of preschoolers (feeling grown up), the emotional needs of young adolescents (*being* in charge) give rise to the emotional needs of older teenagers (*being* grown up). Your role is to help your teenager figure out what kind of person she is and what kind of person she wants to become. At this stage in your child's emotional development, the question on your mind should be: *How can I help my adolescent understand himself or herself better?*

Feeling secure, in control, mature, capable, independent, and self-aware are things that feel good at all stages of life, but each of these concerns is more salient during some periods of development than others. If you keep these stages of emotional development in mind, you'll find that your child is less of an emotional puzzle. And this will enable you to be a more responsive parent.

Providing a Safe Haven

I AM ALWAYS AMAZED by parents who worry about the way their child's physical world is furnished but pay almost no attention to the emotional climate that is so much more fundamental to their child's well-being. I suppose that we are so constantly inundated with advertisements aimed at selling us just the right furnishings for our home that we forget it's more important to create a comfortable emotional environment for our children than to create an appealing physical one. It's fine to make your home comfortable and attractive, but no amount of fancy upholstery, plush carpeting, or state-of-the-art electronics can take the place of a warm and affectionate climate where people treat each other with affection, kindness, and respect. Remind yourself of this the next time you're tearing your hair out over whether you've selected the right fabric for your child's curtains or color for her bedroom walls.

Children need to feel that their home is a place where they can retreat from the tensions and pressures of everyday life (yes, even preschoolers feel pressure from the demands placed on them). Create the sort of atmosphere in your home that allows your child to really relax and escape from his problems. Your child needs to feel that no matter how bad things get, he always has a safe and secure place to come home to. Children need this peace of mind whether they've had a tough day at school, an awful experience on the playground, a day of heartless rejection at the hands of their friends, or a rotten argument with a boyfriend or girlfriend. You can't make these problems go away, but a safe haven at home will provide some respite and distraction from them.

Is your home a safe haven for your child?

Although the main influence on children's feelings of safety and comfort is the relationship they have with their parents, providing a safe haven for your child involves more than making sure that the two of you have a good relationship. You need also to pay attention to the overall emotional atmosphere of your home, which includes the way you interact with your spouse and with your child's siblings. Children benefit from being raised in a loving and happy family where people are kind, physically affectionate, and relaxed. Conversely, they are harmed by living in a home environment that is conflict-ridden, tense, unpredictable, or frenetic.

One of the most important contributors to the emotional climate in your home is the relationship you have with your spouse (or with your ex-spouse, if that person is still in your child's life on a regular basis). Parents sometimes think that how they interact with their spouse doesn't matter as long as they treat their children kindly. But even children who have a good relationship with each of their parents are harmed by living in a home in which their parents are constantly bickering or yelling at each other. When children see or hear their parents fight, or when they see one parent constantly dominate the other, it makes them tense and nervous. Unchecked, chronic exposure to marital conflict or unhappiness can contribute to all sorts of emotional and behavioral problems in children. Children whose parents fight often, for example, are more likely to develop anxiety, depression, and conduct problems than are children whose parents keep their squabbling to a minimum. If you and your spouse are not getting along, try to handle your problems calmly and in private, and try not to let whatever tension exists between the two of you spill over into your family's daily life. If you find that this is not possible, you probably should seek professional assistance.

This is also true for situations in which your relationship with one of your child's siblings is a source of significant distress. You should take steps to deal with this, not only for the sake of that child, but for the sake of other family members as well.

Predictability is another component of a safe haven for children. Especially when they are younger, children benefit from a family life that has an expected rhythm and routine to it. This applies to the small things—like having set times for meals, for bedtime, and so on—and to the big things, like having certain rituals that are associated with major holidays. There is nothing wrong with an occasional surprise, such as deciding to go out for dinner at the last minute or having a special evening in which bedtime rules are relaxed. But keep in mind that children derive more comfort from familiarity than from spontaneity. It helps them feel more in control of their life.

You also should strive to keep outside sources of stress, such as work, from impinging on your home environment. I realize that this has become so much more difficult in recent years because the boundaries between home and work have been progressively eroded by e-mail, express delivery services, fax machines, telecommuting, and the like. But filling your home with the pressures of the workplace adversely affects the mental health of everyone in your family, not just yourself. You may not feel as if you need a sanctuary from the office (you're just kidding yourself if you really believe this, though), but that doesn't mean that your child needs to live inside a pressure cooker all the time, either. A healthy home environment is a calm and pleasant place where people can relax and have fun, not an extension of a stress-filled, deadline-driven workplace.

The same principle applies to pressures that are associated with children's out-of-school activities. It's fine to provide opportunities for your child to acquire or improve skills that go beyond what he's getting at school, but don't overschedule your child to the point where you're creating unnecessary stress. Children benefit from extracurricular activities, but they also need time after school and on weekends when they can just unwind and do nothing in particular. Adolescents who attend demanding schools especially need time to decompress from what often are jam-packed days.

It's also important to provide your child some shelter from the terrible tragedies that have become an all-too-frequent part of modern life. When young children, those in preschool and early elementary school, hear stories about natural disasters, military attacks, or acts of terrorism, their immediate reaction is to worry about their own safety and that of their family members. If you have a young child who asks questions about these sorts of events, make sure that you assure him that this is not going to happen to him. (Children do not understand probability, so there is no point in trying to explain that the likelihood of a tragedy hitting your family is truly tiny. It's better to take advantage of your child's unequivocal trust in you and just give unqualified reassurance.) During times of national or international crisis, don't make matters worse by having the television continuously tuned to the news. This may satisfy your need to know what's going on, but it will likely make your child very anxious. You can catch up on the day's events when your child is in school, asleep, or unable to hear the television. If your child is a bit older, you should ask her if she has questions about what is happening, and you should answer them in as reassuring a way as possible.

Your home should be a safe haven for your child, a place where she feels relaxed, secure, and protected from the world—protected by her parents.

Be Involved in Your Child's Life

Be Involved

What Is Quality Time?

Take an Interest in Your Child's Interests

The Importance of School Involvement

Avoid Intrusive Parenting

Be Involved

HERE'S A little quiz:

- Can you name all of your child's teachers?
- Do you know who your child's best friends are?
- Do you know what he is studying in school?
- Do you know what book she is reading (or if she even *is* reading)?
- Can you name some of your child's favorite athletes, celebrities, movies, and music?
- If your child is a teenager, do you know how she spends her time after school, in the evenings, and on weekends?

- If your child has an allowance or works for pay, do you know how he spends his money?
- Do you know if your child is happy or sad, popular or lonely, anxious or untroubled?

If you can't answer yes to these questions, you are not involved enough in your child's life.

You need to fix this ASAP.

The strongest and most consistent predictor of children's mental health, adjustment, happiness, and well-being is the level of involvement of their parents in their life. Children with involved parents do better in school, feel better about themselves, are less likely to develop emotional problems, and are less likely to take risks or get into trouble. There is nothing more important to your child's psychological development than your deep and sustained involvement. This is true whether your child is an infant, a teenager, or at any point in between.

There is no getting around the fact that, in order to be involved, you have got to spend time with your child. It seems almost too obvious to point out, but I can assure you that I've known parents who spend so little time with their children that you really have to wonder why they became parents in the first place.

One of the reasons it's important to spend time with your child is that you never know when he is going to open up and tell you about what's going on in his life, and knowledge about your child's life is the key to your involvement.

Parents often think that they can learn what they need to know by asking their child questions, but in reality, this only provides a partial picture. Your child is more likely to disclose what's really important in a casual way, when the two of you are doing something together that may be entirely unrelated to what your child wants to tell you. Your son will tell you about a fight he had at school while you're tucking him into bed at night, not when you ask him "What happened at school today?" You'll learn about your daughter's latest crush when the two of you are out shopping, not when you ask her how her social life is going. You'll learn more about how your child is doing in school when you overhear a conversation while driving a group of friends to their soccer game than you will through direct questioning at the dinner table. But if you don't tuck your child in, go on excursions to the mall together, or take your child and his friends to soccer games, you'll miss these moments. So the more time you spend together, the better your chances of finding out what's going on in your child's life, and the easier it will be to be involved. This is easier when children are younger, but if you give it some thought, I'm sure you can think of plenty of activities that will allow you to spend more time with your teenager.

It's also important to be involved in your child's life outside of home. Go to your child's basketball games, piano recitals, swimming meets, and school plays. When she looks out into the crowd, it will make her feel good to see your face, and you'll want to be there to praise her when she's done well or reassure her when she hasn't. Make sure you have regular contact with your child's teachers and attend the functions your child's school puts on for parents. Make your house one of the places where your child and his friends hang out. The knowledge you gain will more than pay for the extra snacks and soft drinks you'll have to stock in the cupboard.

Parenting is not a part-time endeavor. It's not something you do only when you feel like it, or only when you remember to pay attention to your child, or only when your child is in some sort of trouble.

Committing yourself to being fully involved in your child's life doesn't mean you can't have a career. It will probably mean, though, that you will have to work harder to be involved than a parent who is not employed outside the home. The key to using day care and babysitters effectively is making sure that these aids permit you to be more involved when you are not at work, rather than falling into the trap of thinking that these care providers can substitute for your own commitment. Babysitting is not the same as parenting, and you should not expect it to be.

Being an involved parent takes time and is hard work, and it often means rethinking and rearranging your priorities. It frequently means sacrificing what you want to do for what your child needs you to do. It may mean skipping an unnecessary meeting at work or arranging an out-of-town business trip to be as brief as you can afford it to be. But it's worth it. Your involvement in your child's life will give him a legacy of psychological well-being that will last him his entire life.

If you talk to most parents with grown children, they will tell you that they feel as though their child's childhood slipped by in a heartbeat. When your child is about to leave home as a young adult, you won't say "I wish I had spent more time working." You'll wish you had been more involved when you had the chance.

Savor this stage of your child's development. Get involved in your child's life, and stay involved as your child grows up.

What Is Quality Time?

YOU'VE PROBABLY HEARD the term "quality time" mentioned as a way of assuring parents that it's not how much time you spend with your child that matters, but what you do when you are together.

I think the basic gist of this message is fine, but there's some confusion about what constitutes quality time.

Many parents don't really understand what quality time means. They mistakenly get it into their head that some activities count as quality time and others do not. Often, parents believe these activities will stimulate their child's development, such as playing with an educational toy or teaching the child something new. So when they feel guilty about not spending enough time with their child, they pick one of these activities and start in on it, whether their child is interested or not. It's as if "spend some quality time with my child today" is an item on their to-do list, and they're just dying to get it over with, cross it off the list, and move on to the next task. But spending quality time with your child doesn't mean turning every interaction into a lesson about something. Children and their parents also need to just have fun together. You're your child's parent, not his tutor.

Quality time has nothing to do with *what* you and your child are doing when you are together. Quality time is all about *how* you do it. Quality time is defined by your state of mind, not by a set of activities. It's time where you are really engaged with your child.

Here's my question, then: When you and your child are together, are you really there, or is your mind usually somewhere else? If your answer is that your mind is usually somewhere else, you are not spending quality time with your child.

There are plenty of occasions where you have no choice but to parent without being fully engaged. You can't give your child undivided attention when you are doing something else that needs to be done, like cooking dinner, paying bills, reading work you've brought home from the office, fixing a toilet that won't stop running, or attending to a younger sibling who is still an infant. It's natural and perfectly fine when you are with your child under these circumstances to split your attention between her and the task at hand.

But if parenting on autopilot is *all* that you ever give your child, you are not being a good parent. You need to spend time with your child when you are really focused on what the two of you are doing, and not simply squeezing in some parenting while you are doing something else, such as checking your e-mail or reading the newspaper.

Make time for activities where you and your child have a chance to connect. How you do this will vary depending on your child's age and his likes and dislikes, but at any age you can surely find something that your child enjoys doing with you. Again, it's not the activity that matters, but your willingness to get engaged in whatever it is.

Plan special evening or weekend outings that allow you to focus on your child. It's great to take your child along with you while you run errands or shop, but you won't be able to give her your undivided attention. It's hard to create quality time while you are searching for bargains at the supermarket or shopping mall. It's true that you can turn running errands into a more satisfying joint activity by slowing down and trying to make the excursion more engaging, but this is not the same as doing something together where the primary focus is an activity that your child likes.

When you read to your child, as you should every day, put a little oomph into it, even if you've read the same story dozens of times.

When you are doing something with your child, try to get into it, whether it is building with blocks, baking a cake, hiking in the woods, or playing a catch. She can tell the difference between when you are genuinely involved and when you are just going through the motions.

When you and your child are spending time together, focus on what you are doing right then, and not on the chores you are neglecting, the work you have to catch up on, or what you will be doing later that day. Be there mentally as well as physically.

When your teenager is telling you something, really pay attention. Don't listen with feigned interest. When you see him at the end of the day, ask real questions, not perfunctory ones. Perfunctory questions will only get you perfunctory answers.

I'll bet that if you sit down and add up the number of minutes you actually spend with your child each day—not time when the two of you just happen to be in the same place at the same time, but time when you are talking to each other or doing something together—you'll be amazed at how little time the two of you spend together.

How much quality time is enough time? There is no magic number of minutes or hours to aim for. Just keep in mind that the more quality time you spend with your child, the better off he will be.

There are two ways to increase the amount of quality time you spend with your child. If it is possible for you to simply spend more time with your child, try to increase that amount. And if this is not possible, because of work or other obligations, try to improve the quality of time you do spend together. My guess is that you can probably do a little of both.

I know that you've learned how to multitask, but taking care of your child is not something that should be relegated to a side activity. It is better to spend an hour genuinely engaged with your child than to spend two hours with your mind elsewhere. You can be an adequate parent when you are doing something else and parenting at the same time, but you can't be a really good one. Make sure that a substantial portion of the time you spend with your child is devoted to her and her alone.

That's what quality time is all about.

Take an Interest in Your Child's Interests

YOU'VE PROBABLY TRIED to get your child interested in what you like to do, but have you ever thought about developing an interest in what *he* likes? That will give you a whole different set of opportunities to spend time together.

It's great for you to expose your child to the interests and activities that you are passionate about. This creates opportunities for the two of you to connect with each other, reasons to spend time together, and a closeness that comes from sharing something special. Whether it's some sort of hobby, musical instrument, craft, or sport, or even something as simple as reading certain types of books or taking walks in the woods, getting your child genuinely interested in what interests you makes you both feel good.

However, an entirely different way for you to connect with your child is to become interested in what *she* likes. This provides opportunities for spending more time and bonding with each other. It also gives your child a different feeling than when you've engaged her in your interest. Children are so accustomed to following rather than leading their parents that it's nice for them to reverse roles once in a while. And as they get older, children may even begin to teach their parents things, and this role reversal makes them feel competent and mature. (Not to mention the fact that once he's reached preadolescence, your child probably has a lot he can teach you.)

There are several reasons parents often fail to get involved in their child's interests. Sometimes their child likes to do things that the parents simply don't like. (Often, the same parent who expects his child to be patient when he chooses the activity is impatient when the activity happens to be the child's choice.)

If your teenager enjoys watching science fiction movies, for instance, but this sort of film bores you to death, watch a few together anyway, and when they're over, ask him to explain what he likes about them. The next time you watch, look for the things he mentioned—maybe he likes a certain kind of special effect, for example, or a particular actor—and see if you can appreciate the movie for the things your child appreciates in it.

If your preadolescent likes playing video games, but you think this is a complete waste of time, ask him if you can try one with him anyway. Remind yourself that sharing time with your child is *never* a waste of time. And play with enthusiasm, or else he won't be interested in doing it a second or third time.

If your daughter is into music that drives you berserk, stop by her room and ask about it anyway. Listen to what she has on at the time. Ask her to play something from her collection that she thinks you will like, and then ask her questions about it. Try to stay up on what's popular among kids your child's age.

Sometimes parents don't get involved in what their child likes to do because the child is young and interested in things that don't hold much inherent interest for adults, such as playing with dolls or action figures. If you are in this situation, there are two strategies that work pretty well. One is to see if you can stop being an adult for a while and have fun doing what your child is doing. You might actually have a good time if you can let go of your inhibitions.

If you're unable to do this, try to play along but use the experience as a time to watch your child interacting with the world. Notice what sorts of stories she makes up, for example. If your child is building something, watch how he builds. You can learn a lot about your child by watching closely, and you may come away impressed with how skilled your child is.

Parents often prefer to spend time with their child when the activity is one the parent has chosen because it provides an opportunity for the parent to do some teaching. But not everything you do with your child has to be a "learning experience." Frankly, many parents spend far too much time trying to instruct their children, which is often what happens when the only interests you share with your child are ones in which you are the expert and your child is a novice. A certain amount of teaching is fine, especially when your child expresses an interest in learning how to do something ("I wish I knew how to . . .") or explicitly asks for instruction from you ("Will you teach me to . . . ?"). But don't overdo it. It's more important that the two of you just have fun.

There are families in which parents are so busy instructing their children that the poor kids start to feel as if they're always in class. Remember, your child has spent the better part of the week in school. He needs time to be playful and to try things without worrying about whether he is doing them correctly or living up to someone else's performance standards. Children like to do things alongside their parents without being corrected or trained in the "proper" procedure.

A sure way to make your child *lose* interest in what interests you is to turn everything you do together into a lesson. Unless the activity you are trying to interest your child in clearly requires technical expertise to be able just to do the activity at all (such as learning how to crochet or take apart an automobile engine), let your child try it for himself, in his own way, without being instructed, until you sense that he *wants* you to give him a lesson. If you can't sit by while your child does something incorrectly without launching into a lecture or demonstration, you need to lighten up.

I'm sure that if you try, you can develop enough of an interest in something your child is passionate about to be able to spend time together in the activity.

Try not to make spending time with your child something that always has to be on your terms.

The Importance of School Involvement

OF ALL THE WAYS you can be involved in your child's life, probably the most important area is her schooling. So much of your child's life is wrapped up in school, especially before adolescence, that being involved gives you a great window on how she is doing, not just academically, but overall. Moreover, students of all ages do better in school when their parents are engaged in their education.

It's easy to understand why. Deep down, children value what they believe their parents value. By involving yourself in your child's schooling consistently over the course of her education, you demonstrate to her that school is important to you. Over time, your child will come to feel this way herself, and this will motivate her to do well and to take her studies seriously. On the other hand, if you don't attend parent-teacher conferences, take an interest in what your child is studying, or show up at athletic events or performances to watch your child, she can only conclude that school is not very important, regardless of what you say.

It's not just your child who will be influenced by your involvement, though. Being involved also sends a two-part message to your child's teachers. Part one of this message is that you want to be informed if your child is having any sort of problem in school, so that you can work with the teacher to help solve it. And part two is that you are going to be the first one calling the principal's office if your child is not being treated properly. Believe me, there is no better way to show what sort of parent you are than attending school functions and making it a point to chat with your child's teachers.

Many parents think that being involved in their child's education means assisting with homework and other projects when he needs help. Helping with homework is all well and good, but it is not sufficient. There is no substitute for showing up at school functions and having face-to-face contact with your child's teachers.

Let me be clear about something. There is a big difference between being an involved parent and being a parent who does nothing but meddle and grumble. Teachers understandably get irritated at parents whose involvement always takes the form of complaining. But when you are genuinely involved—when you attend school functions, help out when the school needs volunteers, ask informed questions that demonstrate your familiarity with what your child is studying, and comment on what you are pleased with as well as what you are unhappy about—you establish credibility that you can cash in on should the occasion arise when you need to register a serious complaint or make a special request.

So far I've emphasized the type of school involvement that brings parents into the school, rather than the sort that takes place at home, such as monitoring or checking over your child's homework. As a general rule, your involvement in activities at your child's school should remain high throughout your child's education, but your involvement in homework and projects done at home should gradually lessen as your child gets older.

The reason for this has to do with some of the purposes of homework. One of the most important functions of homework is to help your child learn how to manage his time, monitor his own learning, and learn how to make sure that his standards for his own work match those of his teachers. When he is young, he needs your help in learning how to do all of these things, and that's why it's important for you to make sure he allocates enough time for his homework, to ask whether he understands what he's been assigned, and to check that the work he's handing in is done well.

But as your child gets older, you'll want him to take on these tasks for himself. After all, at some point, your child is going to have to make his own decisions about how much time he devotes to his schoolwork, figure out when he doesn't understand something, and learn the difference between work that is top-notch and work that is mediocre. If you remain too involved in your child's homework for too long, he won't have a chance to learn these things. He'll continue to rely on you to do these things for him. So, the older and more mature your child is, the less you should be involved in his homework.

Here are some general guidelines to keep in mind:

When your child is in *elementary school,* your job is to help her establish good work habits. You can do this by asking every day if she has homework, establishing a regular time and proper setting for her to do it, making sure she has completed what she has been assigned, and asking if she needs help with any of it.

You don't have to look at her work every single day, but you should check it over from time to time. If your child has made a lot of mistakes that look like sloppy errors, point them out and insist that she go over the assignment again before turning it in. You want to instill in her the idea that the work she turns in needs to be done correctly , and that everyone's "first drafts" can always use a going over. If it seems to you that she is having difficulty understanding the material, you will have to decide whether you can explain it or whether a better approach is to let her teacher know. (Please don't try to teach her something that you yourself don't understand.) Ask her teacher if there are any exercises the two of you can do at home that will help her understand the material better.

When your child is in *middle school,* your job is to make sure that the work habits you've tried to shape during elementary school have, in fact, become habits.

Let your child decide how much time she devotes to her homework and when and where she does it. But ask every day what homework she has and check with her before she goes to sleep to make sure that she has done all of it. Ask to look at her homework from time to time, but do this to keep apprised of what she is doing at school rather than to correct her mistakes. Again, if you see sloppy errors, suggest that she take another look before she hands the work in. Offer your assistance from time to time ("Would you like me to proofread your paper?"), but don't insist that she take it. It's important at this age that she learn to accept responsibility for her work.

When your child is in *high school,* limit your involvement in her homework to what she explicitly requests from you.

If she asks you to quiz her in advance of a foreign-language vocabulary test, do so. If she wants to rehearse a social studies presentation or have you read through a term paper, be there for her. But once she has reached high school, you shouldn't be asking her if she has homework or if she has completed it, and you should review it only if she asks you to, or if you are genuinely interested in the subject and want to learn about it from her. If she is not handing in homework that is acceptable, her teachers should let you know. At this point, though, she should have learned how to monitor and maintain the quality of her work.

How you respond when your child is having a tough time with a teacher also depends on your child's age. If your child is in elementary school, you need to handle the situation for him. Once your child has reached adolescence, though, your first inclination should be to help him figure out how to approach his teacher and work things out. Follow up to make sure that he's actually done what you and he have decided is the right thing to do.

One last thing: Regardless of your child's age, never correct his homework. It's fine to point out things that need fixing, especially if your child is in elementary or middle school, but let him figure out how to make the appropriate corrections. If you do your child's homework for him, it will be impossible for his teacher to figure out whether he needs extra instruction, which defeats one of the main purposes of assigning homework.

I realize that you want your child to get good grades, but doing his homework for him is not one of the strategies you should use to accomplish this. In the short run, your child may get better grades. But in the long run, your child will be better served by learning how to take responsibility for his work and not depending on you to make it perfect.

Some parents think that it's sufficient to tell their child that school is important. But studies show that the students who do best in school are generally the ones whose parents are actively involved. When you are involved in your child's education on a regular basis, you send a strong message to her that school really matters. When it comes to your child's schooling, your actions really do speak louder than your words.

Avoid Intrusive Parenting

YOUR CHILD BENEFITS from your involvement in his life, but, as the expression goes, it is sometimes possible to have too much of a good thing. Your involvement should not be so excessive that it stifles his psychological development.

Be involved, but don't be intrusive.

Some parents' intrusiveness stems from an excessively strong need to be in control, but most intrusive parents actually have good intentions. They want to protect their child from harm or failure or rejection, and they want to do whatever they can to promote their child's health, happiness, and success. No parent can be faulted for that. But it is possible to go overboard.

Children need to develop a healthy sense of independence, and intrusive involvement on your part can interfere with this. This means you have to learn when to hold back, when to watch from a distance rather than hover close by, when to leave a decision up to your child rather than take matters into your own hands, and when to let your child have some privacy.

To be a good parent, you must accept that there are things in your child's life that you can't control. In fact, part of your job as a parent is to give more and more control of your child's life to her as she gets older. This doesn't mean becoming less involved; it means becoming involved in a different way. As your child gets older, you need to gradually make the transition from involvement via micromanagement to involvement that takes the form of supervision from a distance.

Part of what makes a child healthy, happy, and successful is developing a sense of mastery and self-sufficiency. It's certainly true that your child needs to know that you're there for her, but she also needs to know that there are plenty of situations that she can handle without you. If you micromanage her life in a way that never gives her a chance to do anything on her own, she will not develop confidence in her own competence.

Ultimately, the only way your child can be genuinely healthy, happy, and successful is if you give him the freedom to venture out and make some of his own decisions, even if this leaves him open to being hurt or disappointed. Good parenting requires a balance between involvement and independence. At either extreme— when parents are disengaged or when they are intrusive— children's mental health suffers.

It's important to be involved in your child's schooling, for example, but if you do his homework for him or always correct it before he turns it in, he will doubt his abilities and never know if the good grades he gets are really his doing.

It's important to oversee your child's friendships, but if you constantly intervene in her relationships with other children to make sure they go smoothly, she may become anxious and wonder whether she has the skills necessary to create a satisfying social life of her own making.

It's important to keep track of your child's activities, but if you are constantly reminding him of his responsibilities and deadlines, he will never learn how to manage his own affairs. If you plan out everything for him without letting him have some say over how he spends at least some of his time, you will undermine his trust in his own judgment.

It's important to know what's going on in your child's world, but this doesn't require knowing the details of every phone call or conversation she has with her friends. To feel grown up, she needs to have some things in her world that she doesn't share with you. Being private is not the same as being sneaky.

When deciding whether your involvement is appropriate or intrusive, a good approach is to ask yourself three questions:

1. *Does my child have the capabilities to handle this situation or make this decision on her own?* Look at the task in light of your child's stage of development. A teenager can handle more than a preadolescent, a preadolescent can handle more than a child, and so on. And children differ from each other, even at the same age, so consider your child's strengths and weaknesses. Some eight-year-olds can successfully resolve disputes with other children, whereas others need their parents' help.

2. *If my child handles this on her own successfully, will she come away feeling better about herself or learning something impor-*

tant as a result? Ask yourself what the benefits are of your *not* being involved. Sometimes parents look only at the potential negatives. You already know how to find, apply for, and set up an interview for a summer job, but your son needs to learn this for himself. He won't if you always do it for him.

3. *If my child makes a mistake, will the consequences be something that he and I can live with in the long run?* Don't view every little thing as a potential catastrophe, but be mindful about what the outcome of a bad decision might be. It's not necessary to remind your child to study every single time she has a test in school, for instance, but it makes sense to see that she gets a good night's sleep before she takes the college entrance exam. Let her learn from her mistakes, so long as they don't have dire consequences.

If you find yourself in lots of situations where your answer to all three questions is yes, but you can't help getting involved anyway, you are probably an intrusive parent.

I am not advocating a "school of hard knocks" approach to child rearing. There is no evidence that children grow stronger when they are hurt, develop character when they are rejected, or profit from failure. Generally speaking, pain, distress, and disappointment are not things that children benefit from. But in any situation, you have to weigh the trade-off between the benefits of intervening to protect or help your child and the costs of denying him opportunities for personal growth that come from independence.

And remember, it's not the thought that counts. Even the best-intentioned actions on your part can stifle your child's development if you are too intrusive.

Adapt Your Parenting to Fit Your Child

Keep Pace with Your Child's Development

Adjust Your Parenting to Your Child's Temperament

Your Child Is Unique

Have Patience During Developmental Transitions

Your Changing Role as a Parent

Keep Pace with Your Child's Development

As your child grows and matures, her abilities, concerns, and needs change.

Your parenting needs to change over time, too.

Although the basic principles of good parenting stay the same throughout childhood and adolescence, the way you put these principles into practice should be adapted to suit your child's stage of development. What worked well when your child was in preschool won't necessarily work when he reaches elementary school, and what worked well in elementary school is not likely to succeed when he enters adolescence.

This may seem obvious to you, but you'd be surprised at how many parents refuse to change their ways as their child develops, and then find themselves wondering why they are having so much difficulty using techniques that had previously been so successful. Often, the answer is that what they are doing clashes with their child's needs at that point in her development. Good parenting is flexible, and it needs to be tailored to fit with your child's stage of development.

Let me give you an example of what I mean. When children are two or so, they tend to be very agreeable. Getting your child to do what you want him to do is rarely a struggle. (By the way, the "terrible twos" is a misnomer. This period of heightened negativity usually starts closer to the child's third birthday.) As your child begins to develop a need for autonomy, he will start insisting on doing things his way. A flexible parent will resist getting into power struggles, though, and instead try to use her child's developmentally predictable need for independence to her own advantage.

Instead of trying to break the will of a strong-willed three-year-old by adamantly asserting your authority (an impossible strategy that will just frustrate both of you), you should acknowledge his need for independence and adjust your parenting accordingly. Rather than insisting that he does everything your way, for instance, you can help your child feel more grown up by allowing him to choose among different options (what to wear, what to eat, and so on) that are all acceptable to you. You aren't giving up your authority by doing this; you are using your authority in a more clever fashion. By doing this, you manage to accomplish what *you* want (because any choice he makes is okay with you), but you've also allowed your child to act his age. That's what I mean by keeping pace with your child's development.

To adapt your parenting to fit your child's stage of development, you have to have some understanding of what development is, why it takes place, and what it means for you as a parent. Four points are crucial to keep in mind.

First, when your child develops from one stage to the next, he is changing on the inside as well as the outside. Development is more than just getting bigger or taller. It also involves changes in the way your child thinks, in the feelings he has, in the things he is capable of, in the way he thinks about himself, and in the way he relates to other people (including you). It is true that all children are unique, but it is also true that all children at the same stage of development have a lot in common.

Second, the stages of psychological development that children go through are reasonably predictable. This predictability makes it easier to know what to anticipate as your child matures. Unfortunately, although many parents make a special effort to learn what to expect during infancy, they don't put the same energy into learning about later stages of development, such as the preschool years, the elementary years, and adolescence, or they just put off learning about these later stages until problems arise.

Don't make this mistake. Make it a point to learn about each stage of development that your child goes through *before* your child gets there. Good books and other parenting materials are available for every stage of your child's development, not just infancy. If you know what to expect before your child gets to the next stage, you'll not only have an easier time as a parent, but you'll also enjoy that period of your child's development more.

Third, neither you nor your child can control the nature or pace of her psychological development any more than you or she can control the nature or pace of her physical development. There are dazzling features of each period of development that will amaze and delight you, but there also are aspects of each stage that will frustrate and perplex you. That's the nature of development, and there's nothing you can do about it.

If your baby is waking up during the night, your three-year-old is having temper tantrums, or your teenager insists on debating everything you say, it's not because you've done something wrong and it's not because your child is being deliberately difficult. It's because these behaviors are natural parts of infancy, toddlerhood, and adolescence.

You can learn how better to respond to the special challenges of each stage, but you can't stop them from arising. Development unfolds more or less on its own timetable. You can't rush a child through a particular psychological phase any more than you can force your child to stop crawling and start walking.

Fourth, the same forces that are changing your child for the better as he develops are usually contributing to the parenting challenges associated with that period. Once you understand this, you will start to see the difficult times in a more positive light.

For instance, the same drive for independence that is making your three-year-old say no all the time is what's motivating him to be toilet trained. The same intellectual growth spurt that is making your thirteen-year-old curious and inquisitive in the classroom is also making her argumentative at the dinner table. And so on.

If you want your toddler to be independent enough to abandon his diapers, you are going to have to put up with his occasional oppositionalism as well, because they stem from the same root cause. If you want your teenager to stand up for herself when she disagrees with her friends, you will have to accept that she will sometimes stand up to you, because standing up to others when she disagrees with them is a consequence of her intellectual development. Oppositionalism is bothersome, and argumentativeness is tiresome, but both are signs that your child is developing. That's something to be happy about.

What all this means is that to be an effective parent you've got to get "inside" the mind of someone your child's age. You've got to understand how she thinks, what she feels, and what she's going through at this moment in her development, because it is very likely that her thoughts, feelings, and concerns have changed—maybe even within the past six months.

If you have a four-year-old and can think like a preschooler, for example, you can better see what sort of strategies will succeed and which ones won't.

If you can understand what's driving your ten-year-old's new-found interest in privacy, you'll be in a better position to react to him when he flies off the handle at you for entering his room without knocking.

If you can recall what it feels like to be sixteen and hopelessly in love with someone who doesn't feel the same way, you stand a better chance of saying the right thing to your child when the subject arises.

Some parents object to changing their parenting to fit their child, because they see this as a reflection of some sort of weakness on their part. They erroneously believe that adapting their parenting to keep it in line with their child's development is somehow equivalent to giving into the child's demands.

It's not. Your child's development is an unavoidable fact of life, not a demand that he is making consciously or deliberately. More important, parenting is not about winning and losing—it's about helping your child to develop in healthy ways. Sometimes the best thing you can do is to change in response to your child, rather than vice versa.

You are not engaged in a battle in which the object is to hold firm while you force your child to adapt to your wishes. Trust me, if you parent from this vantage point, you are going to make yourself and your child miserable. (Your spouse won't be too happy, either.)

Be deliberate, but be flexible. Above all, make sure your parenting keeps pace with your child's development.

Adjust Your Parenting to Your Child's Temperament

IT'S FUNNY to watch parents' beliefs about nature and nurture change once they have a second child.

First-time parents almost always are staunch believers in nurture. They're confident that the experiences they've provided their child have made her who she is. They take credit for her good points and accept blame for her bad points.

Having a second child is often an awakening. Parents look at their two children's personalities and realize that they are like night and day—even though they've been raised in exactly the same way. One is always cheerful; the other is easily bothered. One is always on the go; the other is content to sit and watch the world go by. One takes to new situations without difficulty; the other needs a lot of coaxing to try anything unfamiliar. It's obvious that nature is contributing to your children's personalities along with nurture.

All children come into the world with an inborn temperament that influences how active they are, how easily they become frustrated or distressed, and how well they adapt to change. Your child's innate disposition influences the way he responds to virtually everything he encounters.

You've got to take this into account as a parent, even when it comes to the little things. A child who is quiet by nature, for example, will be able to sit still and occupy herself in a restaurant with a crayon and some paper while her parents are having dinner. One who is more active is going to require a lot more distraction while her parents try to eat, and she is not going to last as long at the table. The only way her parents are going to be able to enjoy a leisurely meal out is to hire a babysitter.

This is why it's so important that you understand your child's temperament, accept it, and adjust your parenting to fit it, especially when he is young.

If you know that your three-year-old takes extra time to warm up to strangers, for example, it isn't fair to him if you rush right out when you drop him off on his first few days of preschool or get impatient because he needs a few additional minutes of reassurance before you leave. If you know that your four-year-old is a whirlwind of activity, you shouldn't expect him to be able sit still and play with a jigsaw puzzle for a half hour while you read the paper. If your kindergartner tends toward being fearful, it isn't right to force him to scale a jungle gym as high as his playmates have climbed if doing so makes him uncontrollably nervous.

A wary child can't help being wary, nor can an active child help being active or a fearful one help being fearful. Your child's temperament is not under his control.

So let's talk about what to do if your child has a difficult temperament.

A child's difficult temperament may be a cause of inconvenience for you, but expecting your child to change her inborn nature to make your life easier is as futile as expecting her to change her eye color because you'd like it to match the clothes you've dressed her in. If you don't like the way an outfit makes her eyes look, you change the outfit. And if you're bothered by the way your child's temperament makes her respond to a particular situation, you change the situation.

Don't try to refashion your child's disposition. The fearful temperament your child was born with is not going to change by forcing him to confront stressful situations and "tough it out." Your temperamentally overactive child is not a wild stallion whose disposition needs to be broken. Your child is who he is in part because he was born that way, and you and he are just going to have to learn how to adapt to his nature.

If you are fortunate enough to have an easy baby, there is probably little you need to do to adapt your parenting to suit your child's temperament. But if your child has a difficult disposition, you will no doubt have to make some adjustments.

The key to dealing successfully with a temperamentally difficult child is for you to select and create situations that suit his personality. I'm not talking about abandoning your basic strategies for parenting. I'm merely talking about "tweaking" them a bit.

The most important thing to remember is that if you have a

child with a difficult temperament, you will need to allow extra time when she is facing any sort of change or unfamiliar situation. It doesn't matter whether your child is especially fearful, especially shy, or especially irritable, or any combination of the three. Any of these characteristics require that you take extra time to help her adapt to something new, such as a new caregiver, a new school, a new house, or a new schedule.

The same is true when it comes to experiences that she is facing for the first time, such as her first visit to the dentist, her first overnight at a friend's home, or her first time at another child's birthday party. It takes less to make your child feel afraid, inhibited, or upset than it does other children, and it takes her longer to get these feelings under control when she is frazzled. You're going to have to be patient while she adjusts.

Although you don't have control over everything your child encounters, when you do, try to take your child's disposition into account. If your child has a short attention span, don't plan family outings that require a lot of sitting still. If your child is very active physically, choose activities that let him run around and burn off steam. If your child is easily scared, try not to expose him to things that are likely to frighten him. Just think about his temperament beforehand and use a little common sense.

Many parents think that having their child confront his "demons" is the trick to helping him develop a more adaptable personality, but this is true only for older children. When your child is seven or eight, he will begin to develop enough self-control to be able to force himself to sit still when he is itching to move around, involve himself in a quiet activity when he'd rather be on the go, or talk himself out of being afraid. When he is younger, though, he doesn't have the ability to do these things.

Frankly, if your child is younger than seven or eight, the fewer situations he encounters that bump up against his temperament, the better off he will be. Forcing an active preschooler to sit still for a long period of time will not change his temperament; it will only frustrate him. Exposing a fearful kindergartner to things that are frightening will make her more fearful, not less.

One useful thing that you can do is help your child "practice" being in situations that ordinarily challenge her.

If you have a fearful child who is nervous about attending her first Halloween party, for instance, take her to a costume store beforehand to show her the things other children might be wearing so she can get used to it on her own terms. If you have arranged for a new babysitter to watch your child while you go out to a movie, and you know your child gets upset easily around strangers, have the babysitter come early and spend time playing with you and your child together rather than having her show up just before you are ready to dash out the door. If your child tends to be inattentive, you can invent and play games that require him to listen to instructions so that he can get used to this at home rather than have to deal with it for the first time at school.

There's only so much that practice can accomplish, however, especially if your child is young. So don't expect miracles. Over time, you and your child will discover ways to work around his temperamental vulnerabilities. Until then, it's you who's going to have to adapt.

The trick is to create situations that take advantage of your child's innate strengths and avoid those that accentuate his weaknesses. This requires knowing what makes your child tick, being flexible in your parenting, and treating your child as an individual. These are three good maxims to keep in mind.

I know it isn't fair that your next door neighbor's child is calm, perpetually happy, easily soothed, and able to adapt to any new situation, whereas yours is characteristically crabby, difficult to pacify, or stubbornly set in his ways. But that's just the luck of the draw. Some babies are born with an easy disposition and others come into the world more difficult by nature.

If you have an easy child, you may think this happened because you listened to Mozart, avoided onions, or meditated every morning while you were pregnant. But the truth is that you just got lucky. Be grateful.

And if you have a difficult child, it wasn't your fault. Unless you used drugs during pregnancy that you shouldn't have (alcohol, tobacco, or illegal drugs), it's unlikely that anything you did while you were pregnant had any effect on your child's temperament, for better or for worse.

Don't try to fight your child's temperament. If you work with it, rather than against it, you'll both be a lot happier.

Your Child Is Unique

I CAN'T think of many situations in life where the saying "One size fits all" applies other than when you're buying socks, and even then it's often untrue. Certainly, the saying doesn't have anything to do with being a good parent.

It's true that the basic principles of good parenting apply to all children. But the way these principles are put into practice should be tailored to your child's age, personality, interests, and circumstances. You shouldn't change any of the fundamentals, but you should tinker with them according to your child's personal characteristics.

The idea that you should treat your child as an individual is true even if you have more than one child.

There is no reason why all children in the same family need to be treated in an absolutely identical fashion, and plenty of reasons to argue against rigid consistency just for its own sake. Siblings differ in their personalities, in their talents, and in their interests, and all of these should be factored into how you treat them. Again, follow the basic principles, but tailor them to suit each of your children.

For example, one basic principle of good parenting is that children of all ages need structure and limits. But the actual day-to-day rules you have for your children should vary depending on each one's age and level of maturity. A child who has trouble completing his homework each day, for instance, needs more supervision from his parents than a brother or sister who always finishes assignments on time without any prodding. Both children should have *some* rules concerning getting their homework done, but in this case, it makes sense to have stricter rules about homework for the first child than for the second. Similarly, an older child may be more able to handle a later bedtime or curfew than a younger one, and it's all right to set things up this way.

It's perfectly fine to establish slightly different rules for different children in the same household, so long as you explain why, and so long as the ways that the rules vary are based on real differences between the children that genuinely warrant dissimilar treatment. (It's not good to be consistent just for the sake of consistency, but it doesn't makes sense to have different rules just for the sake of difference, either.)

If your reason for having different rules for different children in your home is based on the fact that one is older than the other, it helps to explain to the younger child that she can look forward to being treated like her older sibling when she reaches the same age.

If your reasoning is based on circumstances that are not immediately apparent to everyone involved, explain your logic. ("You did not do very well in school last semester, and that's why you're not allowed out as often as your sister. As soon as your grades improve, we'll change things back to the way they were.")

I think that parents often underestimate their children's ability to understand the reasoning behind a decision to treat siblings differently and worry that their youngsters will be satisfied only with equal treatment. However, by the time they are six or seven, children are more concerned with what's "fair" than with absolute equality. They understand that fairness sometimes requires differential treatment. Children usually get upset when they feel that the way they are being treated is both different and *unjustified*.

Regardless of how many children you have, it's especially important to permit your child to grow up to be who *she* wants to be, rather than trying to force her into a mold that you've created for her. It's perfectly all right for you to introduce your child to the things you'd like her to develop interests in, but if she chooses not to follow your lead, let her be. She needs to be her own person.

You may be an avid athlete, for example, but your child may prefer to spend his time in other activities. You may have been the leader of your peer group when you were in elementary school, but your child may be an introvert. It may surprise you to discover that you've raised a quiet artist rather than a boisterous ballplayer, but there is a big difference between being surprised and being disappointed.

All parents have fantasies and dreams about how their children will turn out, and that's to be expected. But treat these as fantasies, not plans that are fixed in concrete. Your job is to help your child identify and develop his talents and pursue his interests, regardless of whether they correspond to your expectations. Don't make him feel guilty for not living up to what you had in mind for him. You want him to feel proud of who he is, not ashamed because he let his parents down.

Sometimes our children fulfill our expectations, sometimes they exceed them, sometimes they fall short of them, and, more often than not, they simply pursue a different path from what we had envisioned. I think you'll probably find that it's just as gratifying to be surprised by your child's development as it is to have your exact expectations fulfilled—sometimes even more so.

The problems that arise when parents try to force a child into a predetermined pattern of interests or activities can be especially pronounced in homes with more than one child when some follow the parents' plan and one does not. I'm thinking here of families where a parent and all but one of the children share an interest in a particular activity that dominates the family's time and attention. There's nothing wrong with this, but it's important that the child who has separate interests be allowed to pursue them and, moreover, that she receive the same level of support from her parents as her siblings get. It's not right to deprive her of your attention simply because she has different talents and predilections.

One factor parents sometimes consider in deciding to treat siblings differently is gender, but it's not a good idea to treat boys and girls differently just because of their sex. If your son and daughter have different interests and talents, this may be a fine basis for treating them differently. But don't assume that because one child is male and the other female, they need different types of parenting. The basic principles of good parenting apply equally to boys and girls. Treat your child as an individual, not as a member of the male or female sex. This is true whether you have one child or several. Your child will encounter more than enough sex-stereotyping in life as it is. There's no need for you to add to it.

You also should treat your child as an individual when it comes to school. Parents should have clear expectations for all of their children as far as schoolwork goes, but these expectations will need to be revised as you learn more about your child's capabilities. This is especially difficult in families with children whose intellectual capabilities differ considerably. It's fine to require that each child try his best and invest time and energy in school, but you cannot expect a child whose basic intellectual abilities lag behind those of his siblings to earn the same grades in the same classes.

It's also true that different children don't always thrive in the same school environment. Some children need a highly structured school environment, whereas others need a looser one. Some fit better in a school that emphasizes athletics; others do better in one that downplays competitive sports. If you have a choice of schools for your children, make sure that you choose the best one for each child, even if this means sending them to different schools.

Finally, spend some time with your child alone. Often, the only time parents spend with their children is when the whole family is together. Family time is important, but what usually happens is that the child who is the most dominant or the most needy defines the way the time is spent. It's great to cultivate a strong sense of family membership, but all children need to spend some time with their parents that makes them feel unique and special. When was the last time you did this with your child?

Respect your child for the individual he is and for the unique person he will become. I guarantee that he will thrive from your individualized attention. He's one of a kind, and you should treat him that way.

Have Patience During Developmental Transitions

CHILDREN DON'T GENERALLY develop in a straightforward, gradual fashion. A lot of development occurs in sudden spurts. As your child gets older, her intellectual and emotional development will alternate between quiet periods, when she doesn't seem to be changing all that much, and transitional periods of rapid change, when you'll find yourself astonished by how much is happening so quickly.

It's as if your child's psychological development is sprinting, and then resting and recovering, sprinting, resting and recovering, and so on, rather than jogging along at a steady pace. Of course, his development doesn't stand still during the resting periods. It's just very slow and steady and harder to see unless you look carefully for it. When he's "sprinting," though, it will be obvious.

Take your child's height, for example. During the early years of elementary school, your child is growing taller, but gradually so. If you mark your child's height on the wall each month, you'll see from the marks that she has been getting bigger, but this is a lot easier to see when you look at the pencil marks than when you actually look at her. That's because growth is so gradual during this time that it doesn't stand out unless you chart it carefully.

Sometime during early adolescence, though, her height will start sprinting. In fact, every child goes through a year or so during this time when she is growing literally twice as fast as she was just before. When your child is in the midst of this, you won't need any pencil marks on the wall to convince yourself that she is growing. Some mornings she will come downstairs and you will swear it looks like she grew six inches overnight. After about a year, this growth spurt will end and she'll go back to growing at a slower pace.

Your child has psychological as well as physical growth spurts, and these periods of rapid development can be trying for both of you. The most challenging times you will face as a parent are when your child is going through one of these major developmental transitions.

Because children don't all develop along the same timetable, I can't tell you the exact ages when your child is going to go through these phases, but you should watch for major shifts when your child is between two and three years old, and again when she is around six, twelve, and sixteen. There are "minitransitions" that occur along the way, too, especially during the first six years, but it's these four big ones that often baffle parents.

It's not hard to see why these transitional periods so perplex parents. Children are changing so rapidly when their psychological development is sprinting that it's hard to know what to expect from one day to the next. To make matters even more difficult, development during these transitions is often two steps forward followed by one step backward.

One day it may seem as if your child has achieved some important physical, intellectual, or emotional milestone, such as toilet training, but the next day it looks as if he's lost it. It's not that children lose what they appeared to have mastered. This is just the way children develop: in fits and starts rather than at a steady pace.

Most parents expect some of this in infancy, but it's like this throughout childhood and adolescence, too. You and your spouse rejoice because your five-year-old has finally slept through the night two nights in a row without calling out for a drink of water. But on the third night, he's back to his old pattern and your sleep is once again interrupted. After years of nagging your eleven-year-old about getting his homework done on time, he surprises you with several days of extraordinary initiative. The next week, though, he's back to his forgetful ways.

This "now you see it, now you don't" pattern is especially common when children are going through psychological growth spurts. Between childhood and adolescence, for instance, there's likely to be a phase during which your child will astound you with her maturity, catch you by surprise with her childishness, and frustrate you with mind-boggling unpredictability—all at the same time. One evening your eleven-year-old slams her door and informs you that you're the worst mother in history, and the next day she hugs you and tells you how lucky she is to have you as her parent. She's not being deliberately fickle—she's going through a transitional phase. There's nothing to be gained by pointing out to her that she's being inconsistent, even though the temptation to do so may be irresistible.

This same mixture of maturity and immaturity appears again when children transition into late adolescence. Your sixteen-year-old remembers to stop on the way home from school and shop for the groceries you asked for, but he forgets that he also was supposed to stop and pick up his younger sister, who's now stranded at school after soccer practice. Although your teenager has become more adultlike in many ways, some of his behavior is still very adolescent. This is to be expected.

What's going on? Scientists now know that periods of rapid psychological development are times of dramatic changes in how the brain functions—changes that often involve a major reorganization of the way parts of the brain work together. This reorganization doesn't occur smoothly, though, and remnants of old patterns linger on while new ones are being put into place. During the transition that takes place around age twelve, for example, parts of your child's brain are still stuck in their childhood ways, and other parts are moving into adolescence. That's why your twelve-year-old shows an often confusing mixture of mature and immature thinking and behavior.

If you've ever worked at a company that went through an extensive reorganization, you know that the going can be rough until people have gotten used to the new system. Old habits and routines are sometimes resistant to change, even after the reorganization has been implemented. Certain elements of the new plan occur on schedule, whereas others lag behind, and things get out of sync. Over time, these inconsistencies are resolved, but this doesn't happen immediately.

The same is true when children are going through transitional periods in development.

During these times, you need to be extra flexible and extra understanding. Developmental transitions are frustrating for parents, but they are just as frustrating for your child.

The problem is that what makes these transitions frustrating for you—their suddenness, their unpredictability, and their unfamiliarity—are what also makes them hard on your child. That's why your support, patience, and acceptance are all so important during these times.

One of the most important things to keep in mind when your child is going through a difficult transitional period is that it will not last forever. It helps to look for some glimmer of light at the end of the tunnel. If you look hard enough, you'll be able to see it, and that will reassure you that the phase will eventually end. Just hang in there and find a healthy outlet for your frustration. Don't take it out on your child. She can't help it.

Your Changing Role as a Parent

YOUR ROLE AS a parent changes as your child grows.

Although this may seem obvious to you, accepting this is often easier said than done. Lots of parents can acknowledge this, but not all of them do it without difficulty. Some parents change willingly; others put up a big fight.

Don't fight that your role in your child's life is shifting. Your child's needs are changing whether you like it or not. If you don't change with your child, he is just going to move on without you. You don't want that to happen.

It's easy to understand why parents are often reluctant to adapt their role. We mark our own age in part by looking at our children's age. It's jarring to suddenly realize that you are old enough to have a child who is starting elementary school, or getting ready for her first date, or taking her driver's test.

Not changing the way that you parent is a way of holding on to your child's youth, which is a way of stopping yourself from feeling older. When you continue to treat your sixteen-year-old as if he is still six, it's like taking ten years off your own age.

You may wish you could slow down or freeze-frame your child's life, but this is the last thing he wants. You may be fighting getting older, but all he wants is to grow up.

Don't try to hold on to your own youth by treating your child as if he isn't really growing up. It may be cheaper than a face-lift, but in the long run, it's going to be a whole lot more painful.

There are three specific shifts in the parenting role that prove especially difficult for parents, but part of the reason these shifts are hard to accept is that we tend to view them as losses rather than simply as changes. If you can frame these shifts in a more positive light and understand why it is so important that you allow them to happen, you'll find it much easier to accept and adjust to them.

The first is a shift from being the absolute focus of your child's life to being one of many people your child cares about. When your child is little, you and your spouse occupy center stage. As she grows, however, she is going to develop important relationships with many other people: her friends, her teachers, and, in time, her own romantic partners. (If your child is very young now, it will be hard to imagine her being romantically involved with someone, but brace yourself, because it will happen sooner than you think.)

Your child's widening social circle affects your relationship with her. There will be times when she wants to spend more time with her friends and less time with you. There will be times when she prefers the company of a boyfriend to you or your spouse. There will be times when it seems she values the opinion of some of her teachers more than she values yours. All of this can start to feel like you've lost her.

You haven't, though. It's just that she now has the capacity to have important relationships inside and outside the family. And you're going to have to share her with them. The importance of these other people in her life has increased, but this hasn't diminished your importance to her. She's now able to maintain multiple close relationships at the same time.

If you view sharing your child with others as an indicator of a loss of your own importance to her, you are only going to feel sad as your child grows up. Instead of looking at it this way, try to take pleasure in seeing your child's world of relationships broaden. Her ability to relate well to other people is a gift that you've given her by being a good parent. Allow her to enjoy the gift.

The second change in your role as a parent that may challenge you involves a shift from controlling your child's life for him to helping him learn how to control it for himself. This is a hard thing to accept, especially for parents who themselves have strong needs to feel in control.

Your role will change from making decisions for your child to helping your child make better decisions for himself. This won't happen overnight, but over time you will have to let the balance of power in your relationship with your child shift toward greater and greater equality. When you take your child clothes shopping when he is young, for instance, you make the selections. When you take him when he is a little older, the choices (within reason) are his to make. And once he's learned to drive, he'll shop by himself or with his friends. (Of course, you're always the one who's paying the bill, regardless of whose decision it is, but that's just part of being a parent.)

Allowing your child to make his own decisions about clothes or other aspects of life, for that matter, will feel strange at first, because you will have grown accustomed to having virtually all of the control in your relationship. But this shift in authority is what he needs from you to be able to ultimately become a responsible young adult. There will come a day when he has to make his own decisions, and you want him to be able to do this with confidence and self-assurance. You don't want to have to take him shopping when he is a young adult.

If you view giving up some of your control over your child's decisions as a loss of authority, his growing up is going to make you feel powerless, and that is going to make you feel anxious, angry, or both. If, instead, you are able to step back, watch him become a competent decision maker, and feel proud of his growing ability to manage his own affairs, it won't feel so bad. In fact, it will feel very good, because you will know that your parenting had a lot to do with his competence.

The third change requires shifting from trying to shape who your child is to allowing your child be her own person.

It is fine to want to influence how your child turns out—that's part of your role as her parent. Over time, though, you need to focus less on trying to influence your child by leading her in certain directions and more on trying to help her develop the skills she needs to discover who she is. Your role must change from trying to shape her personality to helping to foster her sense of individuality.

In day-to-day terms, this means encouraging your child to have her own opinions, letting her disagree with you, giving her some privacy, and accepting that there will be things about her life that you are simply not going to know. This doesn't mean that she is rejecting you. It just means that she is discovering and accepting herself. She may end up growing into the sort of person you fantasized about her becoming. Or she may end up being nothing at all like this. Either way, what's important is that you permit her to become who she wants to be.

If you regard your child's attempts to become an individual as a rejection of your influence and values rather than part of a healthy process that will allow her to develop a strong and clear identity, you are going to feel increasingly disappointed and bitter as she grows up. You need to encourage her to develop her own identity instead of trying to impose one on her that you've picked out. If you are able to step back and admire the unique person your child is growing up to be, you'll feel far more satisfied than if you long for the days when she was Mommy's or Daddy's little girl.

Being a parent is a lot like building a boat that you eventually will launch. The building process is gratifying, but so is launching the boat and seeing that what you've built can handle the seas. At some point as a parent, you've got to start getting your child ready to be launched.

Let your role as a parent change as your child gets older. Learn to share center stage with other people who are important to him. Learn to share decision making with him rather than making decisions for him on your own. Learn to give him the psychological space he needs to develop as an individual. If you can do these three things successfully, both you and your child are going to be better off.

The issue is not whether your role as a parent will change: It *has* to change, because your child's development will require that it does. The issue is whether you see these changes in your role as losses, as things to battle, mourn, or put off for as long as possible, or whether you see them as necessary changes that your child needs you to make in order for her to grow up to be a healthy and happy adult.

Accepting your changing role in your child's life is one of the hardest things you will ever have to do as a parent, but it's also one of the most important.

Establish Rules and Set Limits

All Children Need Rules and Limits

Be Firm, but Be Fair

The Importance of Monitoring

Handling Conflicts over Rules

Relaxing Limits as Your Child Matures

All Children Need Rules and Limits

THE MOST IMPORTANT THING that children need from their parents is love, but a close second is structure. One of the main ways you create structure in your child's life is by having expectations for proper behavior as well as constraints on how much freedom your child is granted. It doesn't matter how old your child is. All children need rules and limits.

Some parents are reluctant to establish rules or set limits for their children because they don't want to make their children feel controlled by limits or pressured by expectations. They put themselves in their child's position and imagine what it must feel like to have other people tell you what to do all the time. And because feeling constrained by others feels bad to adults, they reason that it must feel bad to children, too.

It's a nice sentiment, but it's wrong.

Living according to a set of guidelines imposed by someone else doesn't have the same effect on children as it does on adults. The structure imposed by having rules and limits doesn't make children feel bad. In fact, just the opposite is true: Structure makes children feel secure.

If you want to make a child feel bad, allow him to grow up in a household in which day-to-day events are unpredictable, life is chaotic, and there aren't any rules. Talk to any adults who were raised in this sort of a home, and they'll tell you that they would have much preferred to have grown up in a family that was organized and orderly, where parents made and enforced rules and imposed limits on their children's behavior.

Good parents can reasonably disagree about the particulars of the rules they have, but all good parents should have a set of rules that their children are expected to follow. For instance, you may feel that a weekend curfew of ten o'clock is appropriate for a ninth-grader, whereas another parent may think that eleven o'clock makes more sense. In reality, whether your child's curfew is ten or eleven isn't all that important. What's important is that your child have some curfew that you enforce.

There are plenty of reasons to have rules, but the main reason is that over time they help your child develop the ability to manage his own behavior. Although it sounds contradictory, your child's ability to control himself is something that grows out of his being controlled by you. The reason for this is that children acquire self-control by imposing on themselves the rules that their parents have imposed on them. Over time, the control of your child's behavior gradually shifts from being external (imposed by you and other adults) to being internal (imposed by your child herself).

However, if the external control is never there to begin with, the internal control—the self-control—won't develop.

Sooner or later, your child is going to be spending time away from your direct supervision, and you want him to be able to manage himself without relying on you to do it for him. If a six-year-old brushes her teeth conscientiously every night before bed, whether her parents are watching her or not, it is probably because she was made to do this every night when she was four. The reason that one nine-year-old is able to sit still at the dinner table and ask permission before excusing himself when he is visiting a friend's house, while another child of the same age is not, is probably because the first child was forced to do this at home when he was growing up and the second one wasn't. When a sixteen-year-old turns in his homework on time every day, it's probably because his parents checked to see that it was done every night when he was in elementary school. In other words, the rules your child has learned from you are going to shape the rules he applies to himself.

Children don't come into the world with the ability to manage themselves. They acquire this capability by being asked to follow rules set down by parents who expect proper behavior from them and who set limits on what they can and cannot do.

Don't worry about your child feeling controlled or constrained. If you don't manage your child's behavior when he is young, he will have a hard time learning how to manage himself when he is older and you aren't around.

That's what you should worry about.

Be Firm, but Be Fair

IF YOU ARE a good parent, at each stage in your child's development you will establish rules that you expect your child to obey. And at each stage, your child is going to test his limits.

It's what children do.

Infants will cry when you don't allow them to crawl into areas that are off-limits. Toddlers will whine because they can't have candy whenever they are in the checkout line in the grocery store. Preschoolers will complain about limits on their television watching. Elementary school children will complain about doing their chores. Teenagers will debate you about everything.

One of your jobs as a parent is to make sure that your child does what's best for him, even if you and he have a different opinion on the subject. You are wiser and more experienced than your child. You are better able to see the big picture. You can think ahead and not just focus on the moment.

Don't let your infant crawl where you don't want him to crawl just because he cries every time you try to restrain him. You made the area off-limits for a reason, and your baby can't possibly understand why.

Don't buy your toddler that candy bar just because she is throwing a tantrum in front of the cashier. You know it isn't good for her to eat a lot of sugar, but she hasn't yet learned this. Your child's tantrum is not the first one the cashier has seen.

Don't allow your preschooler to watch more television than you think is good for him just because he's nagging you nonstop. You've set limits on his television watching because you know that there are other activities, such as physical exercise or reading, that are better for him. He's not capable of weighing the costs and benefits of a balanced activity schedule. His judgment isn't as good as yours.

Don't relieve your fourth-grader from dish duty and wash the dishes for him just because his sulking is driving you crazy. You already understand that there are things in life you have to do even when you don't feel like doing them. You're there to help him gain this understanding.

Don't relax your teenager's weeknight curfew just because she says she's the only one of her friends who has to be home so early. You know that she'll be a zombie in school the next morning if she goes to bed too late, and, although she may disagree, it's more important for her to be attentive in school than to stay out late with her friends.

When you know you are right, be firm.

Parents who are not firm enough usually are this way for one of two reasons. Some parents give in all the time because it is easier to do this than to deal with their child's resistance when a rule is being enforced. Other parents give in because they can't take knowing their child is angry with them. I've got something to say about each of these situations.

If you are incapable of being firm because your child makes your life miserable when you try to enforce your rules, you are letting your child get the upper hand. You can't let this happen, for two reasons.

First, your child learns that if he cries, whines, nags, sulks, or argues enough, you will eventually give in. This is going to make him cry, whine, nag, sulk, and argue more. Any child can figure that one out.

Second, giving in sends a message that your rules don't matter very much. You want your child to know that when you've made a rule, you've made it because it is important. If you've changed your mind about a rule and decided that it's no longer important, that's fine. But it's important to tell your child this rather than let her believe that the rule still stands but is simply not being enforced.

There will be times when holding the line will make your child angry. You don't like to be told that you can't have what you want, and neither does your child. If you are incapable of being firm because you can't handle your child being angry at you, you need to remember that sometimes your desire to be your child's friend will clash with your obligation to be his parent. When this happens, your responsibility as his parent should always win out.

I know that it does not feel good when your child is angry at you. But if you have confidence in the rule that you've enforced or the decision you've made, use this assurance to weather your child's anger. Tell yourself, for example, that it's much better to have your child temporarily angry at you because you forced him to go to bed than it is to have him all out of sorts in the morning because he didn't get enough sleep. Your child will forget about the dispute long before you will.

It's okay for your child to be angry at you or a decision you've made. It really is. Usually, the anger fades pretty quickly; generally, children do not hold on to emotions as long as adults do. Even if it takes a little longer for your child's anger to diminish than you had expected, it's not the end of the world. If your relationship with your child is basically a good one, a dispute over a rule is not going to affect it in any lasting way.

Let me be clear about something. I am not advocating having rules just for the sake of having rules, or enforcing your authority just because you want your child to know who's boss. This only teaches your child that your authority is arbitrary, and will foster disobedience. You don't want your child to view you as an arbitrary tyrant. You want your child to see your authority as stemming from your wisdom and good judgment. In the long run, that's what fosters cooperation.

In other words, *how* rules are made or enforced is just as critical as *whether* rules are made and enforced. This is why it's just as important to be fair as it is to be firm.

Being fair means establishing rules that make sense, that are appropriate to your child's age, and that are flexible enough to change as your child matures. The rules you make for your child should be ones that you've thought out. They should have some logic and purpose behind them.

Every once in a while, it's a good idea to reexamine your rules for your child. If their logic still makes sense and their purpose is still valid, there's no reason to change them. If your spouse or your child correctly points out that a rule no longer serves the purpose that it once did, however, there's no sense in being inflexible. Being firm is not the same as being rigid.

Sometimes children simply outgrow rules. For example, you used to insist that your child take a bath before bed every night, but now your child is old enough to shower by himself in the morning, and he prefers that. As long as he washes every day, it really doesn't matter whether it is in the morning or the evening. Your new rule should be that your child bathe or shower daily at whatever time makes the most sense.

In other instances, it is apparent that a new rule will serve the same goal as the old one. For example, you used to require that all of your child's homework be completed before she went out to play, but now that your child is more capable of managing her time, it makes more sense to simply insist that her homework be completed sometime before bedtime, and allow her to choose when she does it.

Changing rules when appropriate shows your child that your rules are grounded in what makes sense, not just based on who's in charge. This is crucial, because believing that rules are fair and sensible is what gets children to comply with what their parents want.

Establish rules for your children, make your expectations clear, and then stick to them unless you are persuaded that they need to be changed or unless you decide that there is a need to make a temporary exception. But remember that the decision to modify or temporarily relax a rule is yours to make, not your child's. Make this decision for the right reasons, not because it is easier or more convenient to give in than to stick to your principles.

Be firm, but remember to be fair, too. That's the combination that works best.

The Importance of Monitoring

ONCE YOUR CHILD begins spending time away from home, it's essential that you start monitoring his behavior. The most important deterrent that parents have against their child getting into trouble is knowing their child's activities, companions, and where-abouts.

At any time, day or night, you should always be able to answer these three questions:

• Where is my child?
• Who is with my child?
• What is my child doing?

If you can't answer these questions, it doesn't necessarily mean that your child is up to no good. But a pattern of poor monitoring on your part will unquestionably increase the likelihood that your child will at some point get involved in one or more types of problem behavior, such as delinquency, drinking, drug use, or precocious sex.

Monitoring is something parents need to do both before and after the fact. You should know what your child's plans are before she heads out, and you should know what actually happened when she was away from home.

You should also have an understanding about how you and your child will handle times when there has been a change of plans or when a situation did not develop as you and your child thought it would. I'm a big believer in having children always notify their parents when they will not be where their parents think they are. For instance, if your child had planned on going over to a friend's house after school but ended up staying at school to meet with a teacher, he needs to know to call you from school and tell you where he is. (Make sure that your child always knows how to reach you and how to make a collect call or use a phone card in case he has to use a pay phone.) You never know when some situation may arise that necessitates finding your child in a hurry; for instance, you forgot to tell your child before he left for school that he has an afternoon appointment at the dentist. You don't want to have to search for him in a state of panic.

There is no single correct way to keep tabs on your child. A lot depends on the type of child you have.

Some parents are fortunate enough to have a child who tells them everything without being asked. Their child lets them know in advance where she's going, whom she'll be with, and what she'll be doing, and when she returns home, she gives a detailed report on her activities. If this describes your child, your monitoring job is easy. Be grateful that your child is doing a lot of your work for you, and praise her for this. Tell her how responsible she is for always remembering to tell you what she is up to.

Other parents have children who are happy to share information with them about how they spend their time, but who need to be asked or reminded to do so. When these parents remember to ask, their child is forthcoming. Of course, parents don't always remember to ask.

If this describes your child, you are going to have to get in the habit of asking the where, who, and what questions every time your child is going to be outside your immediate supervision. You need to do this not only at the moment your child is headed out the door, but whenever your child's day is going to involve some time away from you. For example, if your child is generally outside your supervision after school, you should make sure that when he leaves for school in the morning you know what his plans are for the afternoon hours. If you make this a habit, your child will probably start telling you about his plans on his own, at least every so often. But when he doesn't, you need to ask.

As long as we're on the subject of afterschool supervision, let me add that children should not be without adult supervision unless it is absolutely necessary, and that if this *is* absolutely necessary, the best place for them to be when they are on their own is at home, either alone or with a responsible older sibling. Allowing your child and his friends to congregate at a home where no adult is present, whether it is your home or someone else's, is just inviting problems. Even the best-behaved children will take chances when they are with their friends and away from adults that they would not take on their own.

If your child has to spend afterschool or weekend time at home alone because of your work schedule, you will need to monitor him from a distance by using the telephone or by having a neighbor or friend look in on him. I generally think it's a good idea to have a preplanned set of activities that your child will do when he is alone (even if this list includes watching some television, it's better that you have a plan than to leave things to chance) and to insist that you and your child touch base by phone every day as soon as he gets home (it doesn't matter whether he calls you or you call him).

If you have a child who is forthcoming when questioned about his plans and activities but who always needs to be questioned, it's a good idea to do this in a way that demonstrates concern rather than suspiciousness. Don't treat your child as if he's on the witness stand. After all, you're not asking about his whereabouts or companions because you don't trust him. You're asking about them because, as a parent, it's part of your responsibility to make sure your child is safe and taken care of. If you put it this way, most children are surprisingly understanding. It's when they feel that their parents are distrusting that children start to hold back.

The hardest children to monitor are those who are not forthcoming with information when their parents ask. They answer questions vaguely about where they are going ("Out"), who will be there ("Everyone"), and what they will be doing ("Nothing"). We don't tend to see this behavior until early adolescence, but it is not uncommon once children reach this age.

It is hard to know what to make of a child who is not forthcoming about her whereabouts, activities, or companions. I would not jump to the conclusion that a child who holds back information is up to no good, because some children's reticence is really a reflection of their need to establish some independence from their parents, and in adolescence some of that is normal. As a rule, I would look for other signs of problems (declining grades in school, symptoms of drug or alcohol use, chronic fatigue, hanging around with troubled kids) before assuming that a tight-lipped adolescent was hiding something worrisome. But if you have reasons to suspect that your child may be doing dangerous things and hiding them from you, I would ask her directly until you feel you've gotten a satisfactory answer.

Many parents wonder whether snooping on their child—looking through his dresser drawers, reading his e-mail, surreptitiously listening in on his phone conversations, and so on—is a good idea. Generally, I think it is not. A good parent-child relationship is based on trust, and spying on your child is a violation of trust. That said, if you genuinely suspect that your child is in danger—if you think your child has a drug problem, is involved in illegal activities, or is suicidal, for example—and you can't get satisfactory information by asking him directly, you really have no choice but to do whatever is necessary to find out what is going on. But you should exhaust straightforward means before invading your child's privacy.

Don't let your child's uncommunicativeness, whether it is out of a normal need for privacy or he is concealing something from you, stop you from monitoring him. And if your child isn't willing to tell you where he goes, whom he's with, and what he does when he is out, you should not let him go out unless an adult supervises his activities. If he wants to see his friends, he can see them at home, when you are present.

You don't need to know every detail about every conversation your child has with all his friends—that's intrusive and unreasonable. But you do need to know where your child goes, what your child does, and whom your child spends time with. The connection between poor parental monitoring and children's problem behavior is very strong, and it has been documented in literally hundreds of research studies.

Whatever it takes, make sure you know the who, what, and where of your child's activities.

Handling Conflicts over Rules

I HATE TO SEE parents develop the sort of mind-set that turns every dispute with their child into a battle in which there has to be a winner and a loser. That is a certain recipe for disaster, because no matter how the dispute ends, one of you is going to walk away feeling as if you've been defeated. The trick is to figure out a way to settle disputes that allows both of you to feel satisfied (which is not the same as feeling as if you've "won" something).

Some conflict between parents and children is inevitable. You will have rules that your child will not like, and you will get into arguments over them. Some parents and their children argue more than others, but I've never met a family in which occasional squabbling wasn't the norm. If you and your child have disagreements every once in a while, this is nothing to worry about. However, if your disagreements occur more than a couple of times per week, almost always spiral out of control into angry yelling or screaming, or escalate into physical aggression, your family should think about seeking professional help. That degree of conflict is *not* normal.

So the issue is not whether you and your child will get into struggles; you will. The issue is how you will resolve them and how you and your child will feel when you walk away from the dispute. You've basically got four choices.

When you and your child have a dispute over a rule, you can simply assert your parental authority. Your five-year-old won't eat her green beans, so you force her to sit at the table until she's finished each and every one. Your nine-year-old wants to do his homework with the stereo on, and you tell him that he can't. Your teenager argues with you about whether she can quit the school's soccer team, and you refuse to let her. Asserting your absolute power as a parent may resolve the conflict in your favor, but your child will leave the situation feeling defeated and unfairly treated. This often breeds resentment and, at a later age, rebelliousness.

In the long run, overpowering your child is not an effective strategy. You may feel as if you've won something, but you haven't really been victorious if the end product is a child who sees you as an uncaring autocrat. Children, in general, like to feel that their opinion was heard and considered (even if it didn't carry the day), and they are more likely to comply in the future if they believe a dispute was handled fairly than if they think it was not. When your disagreement is over something that could genuinely endanger your child's well-being or future, such as whether your child wears a bicycle helmet or attends school every day, firmly asserting your authority is fine. But I would save this approach for those rare situations in which the decisive action of a more experienced person is really required.

A second option is simply to give in to your child's wishes. Your four-year-old won't wear the shirt you've picked out for him, so you let him wear the one he wants, even if it is the soiled one he wore the day before. Your ten-year-old says she is tired of practicing the piano, so you don't force it. Your twelve-year-old insists that whether he tidies up his bedroom is his business, so you close his door and look the other way. Your seventeen-year-old wants complete control over how he spends his earnings from a part-time job, so you give in to him.

Giving in is fine under two circumstances. It's fine when your child is correct and you are mistaken (which does happen from time to time). Allowing your child to have her way when she has a good point tells her that you are willing to listen to her side and learn from her, and this will make her more likely to accept your decisions when you disagree in the future and you happen to be right. As I've said, I don't see the point of having rules that are unreasonable: They undermine your authority, and the fact that you're the parent doesn't automatically make you right. At the same time, though, you have to be very careful not to give in just because it is the easy way out.

Giving in is also a good idea when the issue is trivial to you but important to your child (for example, how your preadolescent dresses for a party with his friends). Children need to feel as if they have control over some things in their life, so it's important to keep this in mind when you pick your battles. Some parents think that if they insist on having their way over trivial issues, this will somehow prevent their child from arguing when the issues are important. They adhere to what I call the "domino theory" of parenting: that as soon as a parent gives in on something small, her child will start challenging her on everything, even things that are much more serious. Actually, just the opposite is true. When you show your child that you know the difference between something that is trivial and something that isn't, it makes your stance on the serious issues seem that much more justified.

A third strategy is to compromise. You insist that your four-year-old finish a portion of his main dish before he can have dessert. You make your ten-year-old practice the piano, but for only half the amount of time that her teacher has asked for. You let your sixteen-year-old stay out a half-hour later than her curfew, even though she had asked for a full hour's extension.

Compromise can be an effective way of handling conflict with your child as long as the compromise makes sense and leaves both parties satisfied. Sometimes splitting the difference does just this, but often it does not: Compromise frequently leaves both parties walking away from a dispute feeling unhappy. If your child simply doesn't like green beans, for instance, eating half a portion (a compromise between not eating them at all versus cleaning the plate) is only marginally preferable to eating a whole serving. If it takes three hours of weekly practice to master a recital piece, practicing for fifteen minutes each day won't lead to the desired result any more than skipping practice entirely will. If your sixteen-year-old is hoping to stay until the end of a concert so that she can enjoy the whole show with her friends, allowing her to stay out later than usual doesn't solve the problem if she still has to leave the concert before it is over. And more often than not, the next time these situations arise, you'll be right back where you started: arguing about broccoli instead of green beans, ten versus twenty minutes of piano practice, and the difference between coming home at 11:30 versus 11:45.

The fourth alternative, and the one I favor, is joint problem solving. When you and your child disagree about a rule, see if the two of you can come up with a better rule that satisfies both of you. In other words, focus on revising the rule rather than figuring out whether and how to enforce it.

Perhaps you and your five-year-old together can come up with a list of vegetables that she likes, and you agree that these are the only ones you will serve her. (It's a little more work for you, but it will be less work than fighting with her over her green beans every night.) Maybe you and your ten-year-old can agree that she will practice the piano for longer but less frequent sittings, so long as the total amount of practicing she does each week meets some minimum requirement. (As long as her practicing helps her improve, her schedule doesn't really matter.) Perhaps you and your sixteen-year-old can live with her having a standard curfew with permission to extend it occasionally so long as she asks in advance and the request is reasonable. (This actually may help her develop more maturity, as it places more responsibility on her shoulders.)

I'm not saying that this sort of collaboration is always possible or always appropriate. As I've noted, sometimes you just have to assert your authority, sometimes it makes sense to let your child have his way, and sometimes a compromise is an easy and satisfactory solution. For very young children, problem solving may simply be too challenging an exercise. (I hate to see parents talking to three-year-olds as if they have the logical abilities of adults.) But, in general, whenever you can collaborate with your child to resolve a disagreement, you should give it a try. You can always fall back to one of the other strategies if it doesn't work.

Joint problem solving avoids having winners and losers, helps your child to feel more grown up, teaches something about the benefits of cooperation, and makes it less likely that the issue will come up again in the future, because when it works, it leads to a more lasting solution.

Relaxing Limits as Your Child Matures

ONE KEY TO effective parenting is relinquishing control over your child's behavior gradually over time, as she becomes more capable of managing her own life. There should never be a point in your child's development when you don't impose *some* limits and structure. But the rules you make and the limits you set should change as your child gets older.

Some parents become stricter as their child gets older because they worry that the stakes are getting more serious. In their view, it's one thing to err on the side of permissiveness when your child is barely out of diapers, but it's quite another to make this mistake when your child is old enough to get into trouble. To these parents, once a child has reached a certain age, you can't ever be too strict.

Some parents take the completely opposite tack. As their child matures, they pretty much throw up their hands and chuck their rules and limits out the window. They figure it's a lot easier to do this than to be locked in a nonstop power struggle with a child who wants more freedom. To these parents, once a child has reached a certain age, there's nothing much that parents can do in the way of discipline that will make a difference. Why risk the family's happiness over a losing cause?

Still other parents try not to change at all. They believe that they've developed a winning strategy and that there isn't any reason to modify it as their child moves from one stage to the next.

In their view, what worked earlier in childhood should work later as well. After all, they reason, if their parenting isn't "broken," there's no need to fix it.

None of these three approaches is likely to work very well. If anything, they will backfire.

If you become more strict as your child develops, your child is going to rebel, because it's only natural that he will expect to be granted *more* independence, not less, as he grows up. If you drop all of your rules and expectations, your child may end up running with a wild crowd and experimenting with risky and dangerous behavior, because most preadolescents and teenagers are inclined to take risks unless adults rein them in. And if you simply refuse to change your rules, you will most likely be mired in nonstop bickering with your child, because she will feel as if you haven't acknowledged her growing up. Squabbling with you over every little thing is how she's going to show you that she's older than you think.

The right thing to do as your child develops is to very, very gradually ease up on your restrictions, but only as he demonstrates more responsibility. Changing the rules and restrictions you have in place is like driving on an icy road: You should avoid accelerating, putting on the brakes, or changing directions abruptly. The key is doing this one small step at a time and linking changes in your rules to changes in his ability to manage himself.

Each time you ease a restriction, you should watch and see how your child responds. If he handles the additional freedom responsibly, you made the right decision. Leave things in their new, less restrictive state for a year or so before you make further changes. Unless something dramatic arises that necessitates an earlier modification, there is no need to rush the process along any faster than this.

For example, once your teenager starts going out at night, she should have a curfew. But if over the course of a year she has demonstrated that she is able to adhere to this curfew responsibly, you might change the rule governing when she has to be home by permitting her to call you before a certain time and ask for a later curfew on special occasions—so long as she doesn't abuse the privilege. For example, her standard curfew may be eleven o'clock, but you might allow her to stay out until midnight if the concert is running late, as long as she calls you before ten and explains where she is and why she needs to come home later. This change in your rule rewards her for having been responsible and gives her an extra degree of independence by allowing her to decide whether, when, and how often to call in advance and ask for an exception.

If you ease a restriction and your child handles it poorly, you probably went too far, too fast. If, for instance, you were to modify your curfew policy to permit your child to periodically call and ask for an extension, but you find that your child is abusing the privilege (calling you at the last minute rather than an hour in advance or staying out late but forgetting to call in advance), she probably isn't yet ready for the relaxed rule. I don't think it's necessarily fair to reach this conclusion on the basis of one infraction, but a "two strikes" policy isn't a bad idea. If your child has failed twice to comply with a newly relaxed rule, my advice is to go back to the stricter policy and wait for a few months, and then try the experiment again. Just make sure you explain to your child why you're doing what you're doing.

You can use this general strategy for all sorts of rules; just remember to take small steps, to evaluate how your child is handling the greater freedom, and to be willing to withdraw the privilege if it's not working out. Don't fall into the trap of believing that you can't undo something once it's been done. Of course you can.

Before embarking on one of these independence-granting experiments, it's a good idea to sit down with your child and go over the ground rules. Make sure that he understands exactly what your expectations are and what the consequences are going to be if he violates them. Most children are very reasonable if they feel they're being treated fairly and with respect.

Most of the time, easing a restriction that you have in place is going to be your child's idea, but it's also a nice gesture on your part to occasionally suggest something along these lines before your child asks for it. She'll really appreciate that you think so highly of her that you're taking the initiative to grant her more autonomy and independence.

For once, you'll surprise her, rather than vice versa.

PRINCIPLE 6

Help Foster Your Child's Independence

Your Child's Need for Autonomy

Coping with Oppositionalism and Argumentativeness

Give Your Child Psychological Space

Don't Micromanage Your Child's Life

Protect When You Must, but Permit When You Can

Your Child's Need for Autonomy

SETTING LIMITS HELPS your child develop a sense of self-control. Encouraging independence helps her develop a sense of self-direction. To be successful in life, she's going to need both.

Children's interest in being independent from their parents' constraints is rarely something that parents need to foster. Most children strive for more freedom than their parents are willing to grant them without any extra prodding.

Accepting that it is normal for children to push for autonomy is absolutely key to effective parenting. Many parents mistakenly equate their child's drive for independence with rebelliousness or disobedience. Children don't push for independence because they want to rebel against their parents or to be deliberately disobedient. They push for independence because it is a part of human nature to want to feel in control rather than to feel controlled by someone else.

If you consider your child's desire for independence as a natural need to be met rather than as an obnoxious drive to be squelched, you will avoid a lot of headaches.

Clever parents understand that the key to managing a child's need for autonomy at any age is finding ways to constrain the child's behavior without making him feel he's being controlled. I know this sounds hard, but it's really a lot easier than you think. Before I share some tricks of the trade with you, though, I want to explain why your child's push to be independent is something you need to indulge from time to time.

Children need a mixture of freedom and constraints. If you have insufficient limits on your child's behavior, he will fail to acquire adequate self-control. But if you don't provide him with sufficient autonomy, your child will have problems functioning on his own. Without being granted enough independence from you, he's more likely to be anxious, fearful, indecisive, and overly dependent on others. In other words, raising a healthy child requires a balancing act on your part, in which you walk a fine line between setting limits and granting independence. It's an especially difficult line to walk because it is always moving. Where you draw the line changes from one developmental stage to the next because you should relax your limits somewhat as your child matures. But the need to walk that line, to maintain some balance between granting freedom and imposing limits, is always there.

One of your goals as a parent is to equip your child with the decision-making skills and self-direction she will need to handle herself responsibly in the world. I'm not just thinking ahead to when she's a young adult and is no longer living at home. I'm also thinking about times when your child is in school, with her friends, or out and about without you. Her teachers are going to expect her to be able to complete projects that require initiative and self-direction. Other children are going to pressure her to do things that she knows are wrong, and she's going to have to figure out how to stand up for herself. She needs to know how to get herself out of jams when she's with her friends or out on her own. In these and other situations where you are not present, your child is going to have to be able to make responsible decisions and follow through on them with confidence and self-assurance.

I'm always surprised at parents who expect their child to be one person at home and a completely different one with his friends. If you browbeat your child into conformity at home, you're not just raising a child who conforms to what his parents want him to do. You're raising a child who will have difficulty standing up for himself to *anyone*, including other children. Surely you don't want that.

By permitting your child to exercise some self-direction at home, you'll help him develop, refine, and practice the skills you want him to be able to draw on when he's not with his parents. If you don't allow him any degree of independent decision making, though, he'll never learn how to do this.

Now that you understand the reasons for granting your child some degree of autonomy, we can talk about how to do this in a way that permits you to maintain ultimate control while allowing your child to feel sufficiently independent. The five most important components of effective autonomy granting are picking the right battles, preapproving your child's choices, praising what your child chooses, helping your child think through difficult decisions, and occasionally letting your child learn from bad decisions.

Pick the right battles. Don't go to the wall over each and every issue. Avoid getting into power struggles over little things. When your child's choice really doesn't matter, err on the side of granting autonomy. You might want him to wear clothes that are color coordinated, but he has a preference for choosing combinations of clothes that are aesthetic disasters. Unless what he chooses is offensive (a shirt with printed slogans that are in bad taste) or inappropriate (torn jeans to his grandmother's sixty-fifth birthday celebration), let him wear what he wants. He likes to listen to music while he does his homework. Let him. He wants to wear his hair long; you prefer it short. Let him wear it the way he prefers.

Preapprove your child's choices. Children enjoy making decisions because it helps them feel grown up. One way to make sure that your child makes the right decisions is by limiting her alternatives to ones you approve of. When you are in a restaurant with your preschooler, let her have some say over what she orders, but set up the situation so that she is choosing among options that are all satisfactory to you. For instance, if you don't want her to order something that you know she is not going to like, don't ask her what she would like to have without limiting the alternatives first. It's better to say "Would you rather have a hot dog or grilled cheese?" than "What would you like to have?" because the latter permits her to ask for something you might not approve of, which will probably lead to an argument. If you want to limit your child's television viewing to one show per day, tell her which shows she is allowed to watch and ask her to choose among them, rather than picking the show yourself. If you and your eight-year-old are toy shopping and there are some toys you'd rather not buy for her, pick several that are acceptable to you and ask her to make a selection from that group. If you are trying to limit your twelve-year-old's intake of sugary foods, don't have them in the house. That's better than having them on hand and arguing about how often she's permitted to have them.

Praise your child's decisions. You want your child to feel confident in her abilities to make good decisions. After she's made a choice, tell her that she's made a good one (assuming that what she chose was an alternative that was preapproved by you). Saying that you love the clothes she picked out, or that it looks like she ordered the best thing on the menu, or that she picked out the perfect gift for her father will make her feel good and help build her self-assurance. These may seem like trivial decisions to you, but they are big decisions in the mind of a little person. Even when your child is older, it is a good idea to praise her when she's made a difficult decision and handled the situation responsibly.

Help your child think through decisions rather than always make them for him. Sometimes what seems like the obvious right choice to you isn't so obvious to your child. Helping him see why one choice is better than another is better than simply making the correct choice for him. Suppose your child has birthday money to spend and is choosing between two toys, both of which are acceptable to you, but one of which you are sure is going to break the first time he plays with it. Instead of unilaterally selecting the better-quality toy for him, inspect the two of them together. Show him what to look for. Once you've done this, say something like "They both look like they'll be fun to have, but do you think this one looks a little like it could break pretty easily?" Then let him choose. (If he chooses the flimsy toy, let him have it anyway; he'll learn from the experience.) With an older child, too, you can suggest what he might consider when making an important decision without actually making the decision for him. If he is trying to decide among several different summer jobs, for example, you can help him see that salary is only one factor to consider and that it may be worth taking a slightly lower-paying job that is career-related over one that pays more but has less relevance to his future employment.

Let her learn from her mistakes. Some parents have trouble granting their child autonomy because they worry that if she makes a bad decision, she will be upset or angry. Part of what's involved in preapproving your child's choices, though, is permitting her to make mistakes that are unlikely to have harmful consequences. Even this is hard for parents to do because we don't want to knowingly expose our children to disappointment. But part of what you want your child to learn is that being an independent person means having to live with the consequences of one's decisions. This situation comes up frequently when children are trying to decide how to spend their money. You know by now that advertisements are designed to make products look better than they really are. Your child won't accept your word for this. She's got to make some bad purchases of her own choosing in order for the lesson to really sink in.

Your child has a natural need to seek independence from you. Make sure you grant her enough autonomy, but do it in a way that allows you to maintain ultimate control.

Coping with Oppositionalism and Argumentativeness

A MOTHER OF a thirteen-year-old once told me that she and her child bickered so much that living with her teenager was like being bitten to death by ducks. I've not yet heard a parent liken living with a toddler to being bitten to death by *ducklings*, but I'll bet many parents have felt this way at one time or another.

If you were to ask a sample of experienced parents to name the most difficult stage in their child's development, early adolescence would come in first place and toddlerhood would be a close second. It's not surprising. Children are their most argumentative during these two periods. More often than not, these arguments revolve around issues of autonomy.

In toddlerhood, the struggles are over what your child wears, eats, and plays with. In early adolescence, the clashes are more likely to revolve around such mundane matters as the cleanliness of your child's bedroom, the hour he comes home at night, and the amount of time he devotes to his schoolwork. Although the specifics of the disputes may differ between the two periods, the underlying issue is basically the same: Your child argues and talks back because he wants more autonomy than you're willing to allow.

Oppositionalism and argumentativeness are bothersome, but they are natural outgrowths of your child's normal striving for independence during toddlerhood and adolescence, coupled with improvements in her ability to articulate her desires. Now that she has the ability to use words to communicate with you, your toddler can voice her opposition to the constraints you try to impose on her. Now that your teenager has the ability to use adultlike logic, she can engage you in debate.

In other words, a lot of what seems to be your child's increased interest in challenging your every request just for the sake of being difficult isn't really that at all. Your three-year-old has finally developed the verbal skills necessary to disagree with you, and he wants to use them (even if his vocabulary is still limited, it is far more sophisticated than it was just a few months earlier). Your thirteen-year-old has suddenly developed the ability to reason in an advanced way: to think abstractly, to play the devil's advocate, and to uncover the flaws in your own logic. (Some of this contrariness is his way of asserting his individuality, which also is normal during this stage of development.) It's only natural for him to want to demonstrate his new talents. It's not that your child has become more argumentative—it's just that he's become a better arguer.

It's hard for parents to look at oppositionalism and argumentativeness as desirable traits in their child, but if you give it some thought, you can probably see that they are. Frankly, I would worry about a toddler who never behaved contrarily, and I would be concerned about a teenager who accepted everything her parents said without question. To be sure, constant rebellion is not a sign of healthy development, but too much passivity at ages when children ordinarily voice their opinions is often a sign of immaturity. This isn't necessarily something to be overly concerned about unless it persists (most excessively compliant children will sooner or later go through a period of resistance to parental authority), but it is something to watch.

If you have a very submissive toddler you might do a little extra to encourage her to speak her mind and go out of your way to let her know that it's okay for her to have and express her own opinion about things, even if it differs from yours. Every once in a while, ask your toddler what she would like, and if she insists on deferring to you, tell her that you can't make up your mind and that you need her to help you decide. By the same token, during family discussions you should tell an unusually compliant teenager that you'd like to know what her opinion is. As I said earlier, excessive compliance is not usually the thing that drives parents crazy. It's the constant questioning of their authority that is typically the problem.

Once your child has demonstrated her ability to stand up for what she wants, her needs to assert herself usually die down somewhat. This is why the "terrible twos" (which actually occur closer to three) are usually followed by a period of surprising agreeableness, and why the struggles of early adolescence usually start to wane when teenagers turn fifteen or so. It's as if children at each of these stages have already made their point and are ready to move on. Difficult toddlers who continue to be oppositional or defiant during the elementary school years and teenagers who are rebellious during the high school years usually have problems (often, the problems are in their relationship with you or your spouse). If this describes your child, you should probably consult an expert for help and guidance.

The oppositionalism of toddlerhood and the argumentativeness of adolescence are temporary behaviors that fade as children work through their need to show themselves, and their parents, that they are individuals. The right way to cope with this is not to try to squelch your child's desire for independence, but to grant him autonomy in ways that reaffirm his newfound sense of self-direction without undermining your authority as a parent or endangering his well-being. In the previous section ("Your Child's Need for Autonomy"), I suggested a number of strategies for doing just this.

The fact that your child is challenging you is a good thing, not a bad one. It shows that she's growing up. If your child is going through one of these stages, try to look on the bright side, maintain your sense of humor, and just keep in mind that this too shall pass.

Give Your Child Psychological Space

HELPING YOUR CHILD develop a healthy sense of independence requires two different balancing acts for parents.

The first, which I've already discussed, involves finding the right mix of limit setting and autonomy granting. You need to place enough constraints on your child's behavior to help him learn self-control and to keep him out of trouble, but you also need to provide enough opportunities for him to make independent decisions so that he develops a healthy sense of self-direction.

The second balancing act involves finding the right level of emotional involvement. Your child needs to feel that you are emotionally "there" for her so that she develops a sense of security. But you don't want to be so emotionally wrapped up with your child that she feels smothered by your attention. To develop self-assurance, your child needs some psychological space. If you are too intrusive, you will undermine your child's sense of self-confidence.

I'm not talking about being deliberately aloof or withholding affection from your child. These are things that no parents should ever do. I'm talking about constantly hovering over your child in a way that makes him feel smothered. Children need to feel attached to their parents, but at the same time, they need to feel separate from them. Some parents are so enmeshed with their child that they interfere with this feeling of separateness.

To really understand what it feels like to have an emotionally intrusive parent, I want you to imagine being in a relationship with someone who monitors your every mood, questions you constantly about how you are feeling, and empathizes with you so intensely that it often feels as if the person is "stealing" your moods. Of course, none of us wants to be in a relationship with someone who is oblivious to our moods, indifferent to our emotions, and unable to empathize with our feelings. But the other extreme—emotional intrusiveness—is just as bothersome; just in a different way.

Let me try another example. Have you ever sat down to repair something and had another person ask if you needed help before you even had a chance to try fixing it yourself? Or hover over you while you began to work on it? Or watch you intently when you simply wanted to be left alone?

Sometimes, your child just needs to be left alone. It's hard for parents to accept this, but there are times when a child who is upset would rather comfort himself than be comforted by someone else, and learning how to comfort oneself is an important skill that overly intrusive parenting interferes with. I sometimes see parents rush to soothe a child—a three-year-old who has tripped and fallen, for example, or an eight-year-old who has struck out with the bases loaded—before their child has had an opportunity to pick himself up and dust himself off. Often, it's the parent's overreaction, and not the event itself, that upsets a child. If your child is genuinely distressed, you need to take care of him. But sometimes what a child really needs is a reassuring look from you that lets him know that he's going to be okay. Don't let the distress that *you* feel as his parent make him feel worse than he already feels.

Parents should certainly be aware of their child's moods and feelings, but you can be aware without monitoring your child so closely that she feels as if she can't breathe without being questioned or showered with concern. It is normal for children to experience ups and downs in their moods, and only rarely does this warrant special attention on your part. Obviously, if your child is extremely upset, you need to find out why and determine whether there is something you can do to help alleviate her discomfort. But reacting to every passing shift in your child's emotional state as if the world were coming to an end is more likely to make her feel anxious than relieved.

Intrusive parents, in addition to monitoring a child's emotions too vigilantly, try too hard to manage his emotional states, rather than help him learn how to manage them for himself. No parent wants to see her child upset, angry, sad, or frustrated. But you have to let your child feel what he is feeling. You should never try to manage your child's emotions by denying his true feelings ("There's nothing to be afraid of"), by telling him that what he is "really" feeling is something other than what he says he's feeling ("You're not really angry, you're just disappointed"), or by intervening prematurely to stop an unpleasant feeling from developing (solving a challenging puzzle for a preschooler the moment he shows any sign of frustration).

My point is that your child has the right to her own feelings, however disconcerting they may be to you. Telling a child that she is not feeling what she genuinely is won't change what she feels inside. It might make her confused about her own emotions or teach her that it's wrong to display her true feelings to others. I also worry about parents sending different messages to boys and girls about which feelings are appropriate and which are not (for instance, when parents tell boys that they are not really afraid, or girls that they are not really angry). All emotions are legitimate, regardless of your child's sex. The last thing you want is for your child to feel guilty or ashamed on top of feeling afraid, angry, or sad.

Another form of emotional intrusiveness that I sometimes see is when parents answer questions that others have directed to their child, even though the child can answer them for herself. When a visiting relative asks your child how she likes her new teacher, whether she has a new best friend, or what her favorite school subject is, let your child respond. You may not know what your child's true feelings are, and answering for her is a way of telling her that her feelings don't really matter. Again, try putting yourself in your child's position for a moment. How would you feel if every time you were asked a question about your opinion or feelings, someone else jumped in and answered for you, as if you weren't present? After a while, this sort of thing starts to make you feel diminished, and this is precisely how it will make your child feel if you do it to her. Let her speak for herself.

So far I've focused on emotional intrusiveness around negative feelings, but parents also can be overly involved where positive emotions are concerned. Here I'm thinking of those parents who get so excited about their child's accomplishments or successes that their own level of enthusiasm far overshadows whatever enjoyment their child is experiencing. When parents do too much of this, it frequently has the effect of blunting the child's happiness, because it makes him feel as if the event belongs more to his parents than to him. It's important to share in your child's joys, but do this in a way that doesn't diminish his own elation.

It's also essential that you give your child some privacy in her emotional life. If your nine-year-old comes home from school and is obviously bothered by something that happened there, it's good to ask if something is the matter. But if your child doesn't feel like talking about it at the moment, don't press the issue. Just let her know that if she *does* feel like telling you at some point, you're always available to listen. She may eventually tell you what's on her mind, but she'll do it when she feels ready to open up. Your teenager may be all worked up over her recent breakup with her boyfriend, but whether she wants to discuss her feelings with you, her big brother, her best friend, or no one at all is her business.

You can't help wanting to know when and why your child is distressed. But being able to have some personal space, including some privacy, is an important part of feeling grown-up, especially once children approach adolescence. If you can't abide this, you're going to foster your child's emotional immaturity.

Children can't always express the discomfort that their parents' emotional intrusiveness engenders, and they are often reluctant to tell their parents to back off. But having your moods closely monitored, your feelings constantly inquired about, and your emotions shared too closely with another person feels just as unpleasant to a child as it does to an adult.

Be involved, but don't suffocate your child with your presence.

Don't Micromanage Your Child's Life

AT ALL AGES, children need at least some freedom to do as they please in order to feel that they have some control over their world. It's important that you set limits and provide structure for your child, but you need to let her wander freely within these boundaries and decide some things for herself.

Don't micromanage your child's life.

Parents are often unnecessarily directive when it comes to their children's eating habits, play preferences, friendships, and free time. These are all areas of your child's life where you can usually back off somewhat and allow your child to make his own choices.

A lot of unnecessary parental micromanagement occurs at the dinner table. I think it's important that children learn table manners, but this can be accomplished through occasional and gentle reminders, rather than through unrelenting correction. It doesn't matter whether your four-year-old eats all of her carrots before she starts in on her chicken nuggets or vice versa. A six-year-old can be told once in a while to keep his hands in his lap or to sit up straight, but he is likely to forget these things when he gets distracted by the conversation. If you are always watching your child like a hawk and jumping on him every time his manners lapse, you'll turn family meals, which should be enjoyable experiences, into unpleasant times for everyone at the table. There is nothing more irritating than to sit through a meal that is dominated by parents constantly instructing their child on how, when, and what to eat.

Parents should also resist the temptation to micromanage their child's play. With a young child, for example, it's fine to impose some control over his play by deciding which toys are appropriate to have around the house, but once you've done this, let him choose what he wants to play with and how he wants to play. You may like to see him color within the lines of his coloring book, but if he prefers to scribble wildly on the page, let him. Some children enjoy copying toy manufacturers' illustrations when they build with plastic blocks, but others prefer to make their own creations. Either is fine—just let the decision be your child's. If you've given him paints and paper to play with, it's better to set him up at a table with plenty of newspaper underneath than to hover over him, constantly reminding him not to splatter or make a mess.

The same principle applies to your child's playdates with other children. It's important that children feel they are creating their own fun together and not just following a script that their parents have created for them. When your child has a friend over, supervise them, but do it from a distance that allows them to play the way they want to play. Children frequently enjoy making up rules to games that differ from those that have been created by adults, for example, and they actually learn a lot about cooperation and fairness from doing this. You may like to play card games according to the official rules, but there is no need to impose this on children who are having fun playing on their own terms. Naturally, you should intervene when it looks like someone could get hurt, when they seem to be having difficulty working out a problem, or when they specifically ask for your assistance. But otherwise, butt out.

Some parents continue to micromanage their child's social life long after their child is capable of handling this herself. Unless she asks for it, your eleven-year-old does not need your advice on how to resolve a conflict with her best friend, whom to sit next to on the school bus, what to wear to a school dance, or how to tell someone who's interested in her that she doesn't feel the same way. She will derive a lot more satisfaction from taking care of a problem by herself than from carrying out your detailed instructions.

It also bothers me to see children whose daily schedules are micromanaged down to the minute by parents who feel the need to fill every moment of their child's free time with a planned activity. It's not good for children to be so overbooked that they feel stressed out or under pressure. Extracurricular activities and lessons are an important supplement to what your child does at school, but your child also needs to have some free time that he is allowed to control.

A good rule of thumb: If you are managing your child's life to the point where you are turning experiences that should be fun into ones that are unpleasant, you are probably being too directive.

When parents micromanage their child's life, they take all the fun out of it. It's good for parents to be available for assistance, advice, and guidance, but don't overwhelm your child with constant suggestions, instructions, reminders, and directives. You'll turn him into a nervous wreck.

Protect When You Must, but Permit When You Can

IN ADDITION TO having rules that structure what your child is and isn't allowed to do, it's good to have some general guidelines to draw on when your child requests something new or out of the ordinary. In many cases, you will know exactly what to do. But unanticipated situations will invariably arise, especially as your child gets older, that genuinely make you pause and wonder what the right answer is.

For decisions in which you are torn between saying yes and saying no, it's helpful to follow this general rule: *Protect when you must, but permit when you can.*

In other words, in situations where your decision can easily go either way, try to maximize your child's autonomy so long as doing so doesn't jeopardize his health, well-being, or future.

The best way to make your decision is to run through the following checklist:

Is what my child wants to do dangerous? No matter how much your child pleads with you, don't let him engage in activities that are dangerous. This includes everything from riding a bicycle without a helmet, to walking alone through a dangerous neighborhood on the way back from an afterschool program, to riding in a car driven by a friend who doesn't yet have a license. If you can find a way to shape the activity to eliminate the danger, that's often a fine solution. But if you can't, err on the side of caution.

Is what my child wants to do unhealthy? Don't let your child live an unhealthy life. A lunch now and then that consists of junk food, an entire weekend spent in front of the television, an occasional night that runs considerably later than your child's regular bedtime, or an evening when she goes to bed without brushing her teeth will not harm your child, but letting her make habits out of these practices is bad for her health. And, it goes without saying, parents should never allow their children to use tobacco, alcohol, or illegal drugs.

Is what my child wants to do illegal or immoral? It's up to you to help your child develop a sense of right and wrong. Children do this in part by watching their parents, but how parents respond when their children ask about moral or legal dilemmas is just as important. It is rare that children explicitly ask their parents for permission to engage in unlawful or unethical activities, but you'd be surprised how often children talk to their parents about cheating, shoplifting, lying, trespassing, and the like. Sometimes, children tell their parents about their own misbehavior as a means of finding out whether their parents are seriously against what they've done. You should never knowingly permit your child to do something that is in violation of the law or that is otherwise unethical, and you should make your view crystal clear.

Is what my child wants to do likely to lead to trouble? Sometimes your child will request permission to do something that's a problem just waiting to happen. Your fourth-grader wishes to spend the afternoon at a friend's house with no parents present. Your ninth-grader asks if it is all right to have her boyfriend over to your house while you are at work. Your tenth-grader wants to have a small group of his close friends over for a party while you are out of town. Your eleventh-grader asks permission to stay out into the early morning hours with his friends. Most of the risk taking and dangerous experimentation that children and adolescents engage in takes place when friends get together and there are no adults nearby. Don't permit your child to place herself in situations that your instincts tell you have the potential to lead to trouble.

If something goes wrong, are the consequences irreparable or difficult to undo? Your child will make his share of bad decisions growing up, but, fortunately, most of them will not have lasting effects.

Sometimes, though, what appears to be a harmless decision at the moment can actually have far-reaching consequences. For example, permitting your child to opt out of taking algebra in the eighth grade may seem like an innocuous decision at the time, but it may close the door on her taking advanced math classes when she enters high school, which may limit what she can major in at college. (The fact that she doesn't like math as an eighth-grader doesn't necessarily mean that she will feel the same way five years later.) Your child, who is focused on the here and now, is unlikely to think through all the future ramifications of a decision. If your child will suffer in the future for a decision she makes now, you should intervene.

So here's my advice: When your child comes to you with a request for permission to do something new, and you are on the fence about it, run through this checklist. (If you need some time to think through a decision or wish to talk it over with your spouse, tell your child this, and give him some idea of when you might have an answer.) If your child has asked to be allowed to do something that isn't dangerous, unhealthy, illegal, risky, or irreversible, I suggest you err toward granting him permission. If this isn't the case, though, err on the side of caution and explain why you reached this conclusion.

Sometimes, parents make a decision about a child's request not based on the specifics of the situation, but because they don't want to establish a bad precedent. They imagine, for instance, that if they allow their child to watch some extra television one night because he's feeling particularly lazy, he will insist that he be permitted to do this again and again. Or, if they permit their child to take a "mental health day" and stay home from school, she will start asking for this regularly.

I think that worrying about precedents is the wrong way to approach raising your child. After all, you're not writing legislation or rendering a judicial opinion. Every situation is different, and children change as they get older. What may have been inappropriate when your child was ten may be perfectly fine now that he is fourteen.

It's better to be a thoughtful parent than be indulgent or restrictive merely on principle or just for the sake of consistency. Take each situation on a case-by-case basis. It's more time-consuming, but in the end it's a smarter way to parent. It's more mindful, and that's what you're striving for.

Be Consistent

Be Consistent from Day to Day
The Significance of Routines
How Important Is a United Front?
Be Consistent Without Being Rigid
Identify Your Nonnegotiables

Be Consistent from Day to Day

The single greatest contributor to children's disciplinary problems is inconsistent parenting. If your rules vary from day to day in an unpredictable fashion, or if you enforce them only intermittently, your child's misbehavior is your fault, not his.

The easiest way to help a child learn how to behave appropriately is to make her good behavior a habit that she doesn't even have to think about. You do this by being consistent from day to day in your parenting.

Parents worry a lot about how much they should use punishment, rewards, or patient explanation when it comes to discipline. These are all important tools for getting your child to behave appropriately, but your most important disciplinary tool is consistency. You can be the most vigilant autocrat in the world, have the most clever rewards up your sleeve, or have the patience of Job, but if you are not consistent, your child will not be well behaved. It doesn't matter whether you prefer to use time-outs, bribery, or persuasion as a means of influencing your child's behavior. Just make sure that your rules and expectations are enforced consistently.

If your rule is that your four-year-old must pick up and put away her toys when she's finished playing with them, you can't expect her to do this regularly if you enforce it only when you are in the mood to have things tidy. Your child isn't a mind reader. She doesn't know when you're going to be in a straightening-up mood.

If you want your six-year-old twins to stop hitting each other, you need to consistently stop them from fighting. It won't work if you step in only when you have a headache or their quarreling is especially bothersome. You need to intervene every time they start fighting if you really want them to stop.

If you expect your ten-year-old to call you at work every day as soon as he gets home from school, he won't do this reliably if you let him slip once or twice each week. You want to be consistent enough in your expectation that his calling you becomes habitual.

If you've told your twelve-year-old that she's allowed to spend only one hour per day on the Internet, don't let this hour gradually increase without your permission. Before you know it, she'll be online for three hours every day instead of the one that you had limited her to.

If you have told your newly licensed teenage driver that he's not allowed to drive with friends in the car until he's had his license for at least six months (a very good idea, by the way, because teenage passengers increase the risk of an inexperienced driver having an accident), you can't look the other way when the passengers are the friends of his that you like but enforce the rule when they are teenagers you've never met.

Often, a parent is inconsistent without even being aware of it. If you are having a difficult time disciplining your child, the first thing you should do is step back and ask yourself whether the problem is inconsistency. Look at this possibility before considering other explanations.

There are many causes of inconsistent parenting, but the most significant is probably stress. When you are under a lot of stress, regardless of the source, it's easy to be distracted and to lose focus as a parent. This happens frequently when parents are going through a significant change (for example, a separation, divorce, or remarriage, or a major residential relocation) and when a family is having a tough time financially. If your family is going through one of these changes, you should make extra efforts to be consistent in your behavior toward your child.

It is amazing how rapidly children's misbehavior turns around once their parents make a conscious effort to enforce their rules in a reliable fashion. If you are having problems getting your child to comply with your wishes, it usually will take only a couple of weeks of clear and consistent discipline to create a dramatic improvement around your house.

The Significance of Routines

IT'S MUCH EASIER for parents to be consistent in their discipline when their family life is organized than when it is haphazard. When life is too unpredictable, it is easy to get distracted, and distracted parents are often inconsistent.

Consistency in your daily routines will breed consistency in your parenting.

Try to have set routines that regulate the daily rhythms of your household. As much as possible, your family should eat meals at regular times; follow the same routines for recurring tasks, such as getting your children dressed, to and from school, and ready for bed; and go to sleep and wake up at more or less the same time each day (having regular sleep times is healthy for both children and adults). It's fine to relax these routines a bit on weekends, but bear in mind that the further you veer from your weekday schedule on Saturdays and Sundays, the harder it will be for your child to make the transition back to the weekday schedule on Monday morning.

It's especially important that you keep your child's bedtime the same every night, unless unusual circumstances make it impossible (you are visiting family friends, and the evening lasts longer than you had expected) or necessary (there is a show playing in town that you promised your child you would take her to see that runs past her normal bedtime). Having a consistent bedtime that permits your child to get sufficient sleep will make your job as a parent much easier. Sleep-deprived children are often irritable and difficult to discipline effectively.

As long as we're discussing bedtimes, let me say a few words about the sleep patterns of teenagers. This is an issue that frequently creates a lot of conflict between parents and teens.

Your brain has an internal "clock" that creates a regular cycle of sleepiness and wakefulness every day. You may be a morning person or an evening person, but whichever you are, you probably have certain times of day when you typically feel wide awake and others when you usually feel drowsy.

Scientists have found that after children go through puberty there is a biological change in their brain's clock that makes it more difficult for them to fall asleep at night. When their regular bedtime rolls around, they feel exactly as you do when you try to force yourself to sleep when you aren't tired. The problem is that when teenagers stay up late, it is difficult for them to wake up early, and, as a consequence, they often are half-asleep during the morning hours of school.

You can combat your adolescent's natural tendency to want to stay up late by forcing him to get up early every day of the week; if done regularly, this will override the biological shift in his internal clock. But this has to be done consistently to be effective. If you force your teenager to get up early on school days but allow him to sleep until noon on Saturdays and Sundays, you will undo the override, and it will be extremely difficult for him to get up early the next few mornings.

Keep in mind that the key factor in regulating your child's internal clock is the time he *wakes up*, not when he goes to sleep. In other words, you can let your teenager stay up as late as he wants on weekends, as long as you insist that he get out of bed around the same time he needs to get up on school days. Be prepared for a fight about the consistent wake-up time, but bear in mind that if your teenager is a walking zombie on Monday and Tuesday mornings, sleeping in on weekends is the likely cause. You'll have to decide whether correcting this is worth the struggle it may provoke.

Whether they pertain to bedtimes or bath times meal times or study times, routines help families function more effectively. Familiar routines make children feel safe and secure, because they feel more in control when they know what to expect. This is why young children often insist that their parents follow the same rituals. If your three-year-old's bedtime routine is a bath, followed by two stories, and then a lullaby, she will not like it if one night you change things and start your singing after the first story. She's going to correct you and tell you that you forgot to read the second one, and she won't want to hear the lullaby until you do. (If you are pressed for time when putting your child to bed, it's better to stick to the routine and make each component shorter than to leave anything out.)

The feeling of security that children derive from routines lessens somewhat as they get older and gain more control over their life, and, naturally, it is harder to maintain family routines once your child has become immersed in afterschool, weekend, and evening activities that complicate your family's schedule. But even during adolescence, it is good to maintain a certain amount of regularity in the way your home functions from day to day. It helps establish a rhythm that makes your house feel calmer. And that makes being a consistent parent a lot easier.

How Important Is a United Front?

ONE OF THE most frequent questions parents ask is whether it's important for spouses to maintain a united front in matters of discipline.

The simplest answer is that it depends on your child's age. The younger your child is, the more important it is for spouses to be consistent with each other. This is true regardless of whether you are married, separated, divorced, or remarried.

Young children (those six and younger) are easily confused when one parent has different rules from the other, or when one parent enforces rules and the other does not. At this age, children tend to see the world in absolute terms. Because they have a hard time resolving discrepancies between two opposing views, they can't understand why Dad says one thing and Mom says something else. To them, there can be only one "right" way to do things. This is a problem when you and your spouse don't present a united front, because you don't want your child to see one of you as the right parent and the other as the wrong one. Over time, this will only undermine your child's respect for the parent who is typically on the wrong side of things.

The need to see the world in such black-and-white terms gradually disappears between the ages of six and eleven. My advice is that if your child is not yet eleven or so, you and your spouse should do what you can to present a united front. It will make life a lot easier for your child if you work out your disagreements and keep them private.

A united front is certainly desirable when you have older children or teenagers, but it isn't absolutely necessary. Once they have turned eleven or twelve, children understand that people can disagree about things without either of them being wrong. They will usually attribute differences in their parents' behavior to differences in their personalities or values. Instead of seeing one parent as right and the other as wrong, for example, children at this age will come to view one parent as strict and the other as lenient. Of course, this can create a different set of problems; a clever child will soon learn to approach the lenient parent first when asking permission for something and to play one parent against the other. But, by and large, this is something you can probably handle if you follow the advice contained in this section.

If you and your spouse have differences of opinion over how to handle a particular disciplinary issue, the first step is to talk it through outside the earshot of your child. (This is a good idea regardless of your child's age.)

If your disagreement surfaces in front of the child (for example, you and your spouse are watching television when your preadolescent enters the room, asks permission to have his ear pierced, and you are shocked to hear your spouse say it's okay), it's fine to tell your child that you need to talk it over before making a final decision. This is less awkward when neither of you has actually voiced an opinion yet, but even if one or both of you have, there's no harm in saying that the two of you disagree and need to discuss things. Whatever you do, though, don't try to work out your difference of opinion while your child is standing there waiting. You have no idea whether the discussion will be short, simple, and calm, or long, complicated, and heated. It's fine for your child to be exposed to the former, but you don't want him to be exposed to the latter.

When you and your spouse finally have a chance to discuss the matter, try hard to find common ground and understand each other's perspective on the issue. Step away from the specifics of the matter at hand and see whether one of you has taken a stance that is more consistent with the principles you've been trying to follow. This will help you see what the real issue is.

Sometimes, one of you is simply too close to the details of the issue to look at it objectively. If you can't find a solution that is acceptable to both of you, and if the decision doesn't have to be made immediately, set the matter aside and revisit it later or the following day. One of you may change your opinion.

There will invariably be issues on which the two of you simply cannot agree, even after a thorough discussion. In these cases, you are just going to have to "agree to disagree," pick a solution, and go with it. Few decisions are cast in stone, and if you find you've made a mistake, you can always change your mind.

Agreeing to disagree is not a problem. It's more important that you do the right thing than that you be consistent with each other just for the sake of agreement. Children fare better when at least one of their parents follows the principles of effective parenting than when their parents force themselves to agree with each other but happen to be wrong.

When you and your spouse are both technically correct, but still don't agree, you can usually reconcile hard-to-resolve disagreements on one of several grounds:

- *Decide on the basis of which parent the issue is more important to.* If you don't care all that much, it makes no sense to stand on principle. There will be times when the situation is reversed, and you'll appreciate being given extra consideration when you feel more strongly than your spouse does.

- *Err on the side of caution.* It is a lot easier for a lenient parent to live with a cautious decision than vice versa. It is also usually the safer bet as far as your child is concerned. If you want to relax your child's curfew but your spouse does not, you should probably follow your spouse's instinct.

• *Decide on the basis of which one of you has more relevant expertise.* If the issue concerns your child's physical health, and one of you is a physician, that parent is probably in a better position to make a decision.

• *Decide on the basis of which parent is going to bear the brunt of the decision.* If what you decide will affect your spouse's daily routine but not yours (perhaps a decision will mean that your spouse is going to have to spend extra hours each week shuttling your child around), give your spouse more say.

• *When all else fails, decide on the basis of equity between the two of you.* If virtually all of your recent decisions have favored one person's view, it's probably time to even things out a bit.

Once you have worked things out with your spouse, it's important that you support each other, even if you disagree with the final decision.

Supporting each other is not the same as presenting a united front.

If your child is old enough to understand that two people can disagree and both be right, there's no problem in telling your child that the two of you disagree but have made a decision on some other basis (it is the safer option, it mattered much more to one parent than the other, it will make one parent's life easier, and so on). This will teach your child important lessons about the need for compromise in healthy relationships. She will not learn this if you present a united front every time you disagree.

However, supporting each other means that even if you and

your spouse do not see eye to eye, you will not undermine either the decision or your spouse's authority by helping your child work around the policy, by winking at your child when you know he's violated it, by knowingly failing to enforce it when your spouse is not around, or by suggesting to your child, implicitly or explicitly, that you are on his side but that your spouse is not.

This sort of sabotage happens frequently when separated or divorced parents are having trouble working out their differences amicably, but it happens in married households as well, usually when one parent is too insecure in the parenting role to bear making a child angry. These secret or unspoken alliances between a child and one parent are harmful, because they either undermine the authority of the other parent or make the child feel guilty for doing what he's been explicitly told not to do. When they are younger, children may favor the "nice" parent in these situations, but in the long run, most children will grow up appreciating the parent who behaved responsibly and have less respect for the parent who behaved more like a child than an adult.

If your child is angry at you because the decision you came to didn't turn out the way he had hoped, and you were the insistent parent, don't worry about it. This is not a problem as long as one parent is not habitually forced into the role of the "bad guy," and as long as your decision pleases your child every once in a while. If a child is always being told no and the blame is always placed on the same parent's shoulders, he is bound to become resentful toward that parent.

When you and your spouse don't agree, don't get drawn into a power struggle over it. This is not a battle to see who's the stronger, smarter, kinder, or better parent. The correct resolution to any disagreement you have with your spouse is the one that is best for your child, not the one that establishes one parent's authority over the other's. Parenting is not a competition.

Be Consistent Without Being Rigid

BEING CONSISTENT in the way you discipline your child is not the same thing as being rigid. Good parents are flexible without being inconsistent.

The difference between being consistent and being rigid is that consistent discipline is adapted to fit the situation, whereas rigid discipline is the same regardless of circumstances. This sort of inflexibility is foolish and serves no purpose other than to assert your authority over your child. As I've explained, telling your child who's boss is not the reason to have rules. Rules exist to help guide your child's behavior, and intelligent guidance requires sizing up the situation and acting accordingly.

Inflexibility over rules takes many forms. For instance, some parents generally insist that each and every rule be enforced down to the letter, regardless of the situation. To them, any violation of a rule or expectation, no matter what the circumstances, is inexcusable. A preschooler has been told that he cannot have dessert until he finishes all of his main course; this is what's required every single night, regardless of whether what was served is something he absolutely detests. A fifth-grader is expected to do her homework as soon as she gets home from school; when her friend calls to ask for advice about handling a problem with another girl, she is forced to tell her friend that she will return the call later. A teenager has been given a weekly chore that is expected to be completed by noon on Saturday; she will suffer the consequences if she hasn't finished it by two o'clock, even if she is late in getting to it because she has gotten caught up in a book, and even though it doesn't really matter when the job is done.

Reasonable exceptions to your rules do not undermine your authority, they strengthen it, because they show that your rules are thoughtful and not arbitrary. A preschooler won't fall ill if every once in a while his parents let him partially skip the main part of a meal and go straight to dessert. (Actually, the more you turn dessert into a special prize, the more intensely a child will want it.) A fifth-grader can delay doing her math problems until after dinner to help counsel a friend in need. (It's just as important that your child develop social skills as it is that she develop academic ones.) A teenager is old enough to estimate how long it will take to complete a chore and figure out how much time she has before she needs to start. (Besides, why interrupt a teenager's reading if the chore can wait?)

Inflexibility over rules takes other forms as well. Some parents are so rigid that they are unwilling to consider changing rules that are wrong or not working. A five-year-old has difficulty falling asleep every night because she's being put too bed too early, but her parents insist on sticking to a bedtime that she may have simply outgrown. An eight-year-old is not allowed to walk by himself to a neighbor's house, even though the neighborhood is safe and all of his same-age neighborhood friends are permitted to roam from house to house. A twelve-year-old is not permitted to go to the movies in a group of boys and girls without an adult present, yet this is a very common social activity in her grade at school.

It is not inconsistent to revise rules when you realize that they might be wrong or developmentally inappropriate. It's sensible.

Extending a five-year-old's bedtime by a half hour may make putting her to bed enormously easier and still permit her to get enough sleep. Checking with other careful parents who live nearby may reveal that the neighborhood is safe enough for someone your child's age to walk to his friends' homes. Permitting your twelve-year-old to go on group dates, but insisting that she is dropped off and picked up right before and immediately after the movie, allows her to socialize with her friends in an age-appropriate way but allows her parents to exercise some control over where and how she spends her free time.

Every parent inevitably makes some rules that turn out to be bad ones. But it makes no sense to stick with a rule that is obviously not accomplishing what you'd intended just to avoid going back on your word or admitting that you had made a mistake. When one of your rules is not resulting in the goal you've sought to achieve, despite its consistent enforcement, step back from the specific situation and think about what it is that the rule is supposed to accomplish. There almost always is another way to reach the same goal. In other words, your intentions may be fine, but you may have to find another way to achieve them.

Another part of being flexible is focusing on your child's intent, and not on his behavior. Children sometimes break rules inadvertently or with genuinely good intentions. Before you reprimand your child, make sure you find out *why* he did what he did.

Your six-year-old has broken a vase in a room in which he wasn't permitted to play because he was trying to wrestle one of his stuffed animals away from the family dog, which had run into the room. (It's easy for a six-year-old to get caught up in the moment, and he was worried that you would be angry if his toy were damaged.) Your ten-year-old used your computer when you weren't home because he needed to access the Internet to research a school project due the next day; now he's accidentally deleted a file you had been working on because he didn't check to see if anything needed saving before turning the computer off. (He had forgotten that turning a computer off loses any work that had not been saved.) Your teenager didn't call and let you know that she was going to be home late because she and her friends were stuck in postconcert parking lot traffic and she had forgotten to charge her cell phone before leaving the house. (Teenagers are not as good at planning ahead as adults are.)

The appropriate way to respond to a child who has broken a rule for understandable reasons is to explain what he might have done differently or what he should do the next time the situation arises (entice the dog out of the room and away from things that could break, call you at the office before using your computer, stop at the first pay phone and explain the delay). When making decisions about discipline, it's your child's motives, not his actions, that really matter.

Be consistent without being rigid. In the end, you'll get better behavior from your child by being appropriately flexible than by being irrationally unbending.

Identify Your Nonnegotiables

IN TRYING TO decide when to be flexible and when to be firm, it helps to have an idea of what your "nonnegotiables" are. Nonnegotiables are rules that you've established that are so important that it is perfectly appropriate to enforce them in an uncompromising way.

It's not my place to tell you what your nonnegotiables should be, because this will depend on your child's age, your family's circumstances, and your personal values. What might be a nonnegotiable when your child is young (calling and asking permission before going to a friend's house after school) might be a rule you relax when your child is older (your child doesn't need to call beforehand, but she needs to call once she's gotten there to let you know where she is). What might be a nonnegotiable to a family living in a crime-ridden neighborhood (never walking home from school alone) might be open for discussion for a family living in a less dangerous community (where walking home alone during daylight is perfectly safe). What might be a nonnegotiable to a religious family (going to religious services each week) might not be to one for whom religion is less important (your child decides whether and when to accompany you).

Your list of nonnegotiables should be short and should include only rules that affect your child's safety and health, involve an illegal behavior, or involve a deeply held family value or tradition.

As an exercise, it might be interesting to sit down, either alone or with your spouse, and think through what might fall into the nonnegotiable category for you.

I'm not of the view that taking an unyielding stance on more minor issues (what your child wears, how neatly your child keeps his room, what music your child listens to, whether his hair is long or short) makes it easier to hold firm when a great deal more is at stake. Some parents believe this to be true, but I think that just the opposite is the case. If you show open-minded flexibility on relatively less important matters, you child will really get your point when you refuse to bend on the significant ones.

This is especially true once your child gets to be about ten or eleven, when he starts to understand the difference between issues that are merely matters of taste (and where it feels "unfair" for you to have unilateral control over his decisions) and issues that are legitimately governed by your authority (and where, like it or not, you can at least agree that this is a decision that you have a right to decide).

I'm not suggesting that it's your child who should be deciding whether your authority is legitimate. But understanding how children think about these things will help you be a better parent and will cut down on unnecessary bickering and squabbling. You'll be surprised to know, for instance, that children actually do make distinctions between issues they think they should have some say about and those they do not, and that your child is far less likely to challenge you if the issue is one that involves serious consequences (for example, cigarette smoking) than if the issue is one whose consequences are trivial (for example, coloring one's hair). Many of the parental nonnegotiable issues that preadolescents and adolescents argue over shouldn't even be in this category.

Know what your nonnegotiables are, but don't make the list any longer than absolutely necessary. The more your authority is based on wisdom and not power, the less your child will challenge it.

Avoid Harsh Discipline

Should Children Be Punished?
Never Use Physical Punishment
Don't Be Verbally Abusive
Controlling Your Anger
The Right Way to Punish

Should Children Be Punished?

THERE ARE ONLY three basic ways to get your child to change his behavior when he's done something you disapprove of: punish him, reward him for some desirable alternative behavior, or explain why what he did was wrong and tell him how you'd like him to behave the next time.

For example, if your child has been pulling on the cat's tail and you want him to stop, you can punish him every time he pulls it, reward him every time he plays with the cat nicely, or explain to him why it hurts the cat when he pulls its tail and ask him not to do it again. If done correctly, all of these will probably work to some degree.

Most parents end up using a combination of punishment, reward, and explanation, depending on the circumstances, the child's age, and the nature of the misbehavior.

Even if you are adamantly opposed to using punishment on principle, there will be times when reward or explanation alone aren't practical, or when you have tried them but been unsuccessful. So even if you are the type of parent who wants to use punishment only sparingly, you still need to understand how and why it works.

There is no truth to the idea that punishment is inherently bad for children or that it is less effective than using reward or explanation. The important question about punishment, or about almost any disciplinary technique, for that matter, is not *whether* the technique should be used, but *when* and *how*. Punishment, reward, and explanation can all be effective if they are done properly, but all of them can be ineffective if they aren't.

There are many ways to punish a child, and they all fall into one of two categories. The first category is what psychologists call "power assertion." Power assertion is just what it sounds like: punishment that is based on the power advantage you have over your child. If you spank your child, yell at her, put her on a time-out, take away her favorite toy, or send her to her room without dessert, you are using power assertion. Some forms of power assertion are fine to use (time-out, deprivation of privileges), others (spanking, yelling) are not, for reasons I explain in the next two sections ("Never Use Physical Punishment" and "Don't Be Verbally Abusive").

The other broad category of punishment is what psychologists call "love withdrawal." This isn't exactly what it sounds like, because you aren't necessarily withdrawing love when you punish your child this way. Love withdrawal refers to any type of punishment that is based on making your child feel sad, guilty, or ashamed for having disappointed or angered you. When you give your child the silent treatment, act cold or aloof out of anger, tell your child that you arc upset at what he did, or tell him that he's let you down, you are using love withdrawal. As in the case of power assertion, there are acceptable forms of love withdrawal (telling your child that what he did disappointed you) and ones that you should not use (telling your child that you are embarrassed to be his parent).

Understanding the difference between power assertion and love withdrawal is the first step in using punishment effectively, because the two approaches work for different reasons. Once you understand this, you'll better appreciate when one approach is going to be more effective than the other.

Power assertion is effective only if you have power over your child. This is why many forms of power assertion work only when your child is young. For example, raising your voice to your child when she is four may be effective because anger from a more powerful person is frightening, but doing so when she is fourteen is unlikely to have any effect, because at that age she's too old to be afraid of your screaming.

Therefore, as your child gets older, power assertion becomes a less and less effective way of disciplining your child. I know this sounds too obvious to be helpful, but based on the number of parents I've seen screaming at their teenagers, it's clear that a lot of parents don't understand that you can't assert power over an older child in the same way you can over a younger one.

Love withdrawal works only if your child cares enough about you and your relationship to feel guilty, sad, or ashamed when she knows that you are upset or disappointed. If you and your child are very close, love withdrawal will be very effective— at any age—in getting her to stop what you want her to stop doing. If you and your child are distant, though, acting aloof is a waste of time. If your child doesn't really care about pleasing you, your disappointment will not make her feel guilty or sorry. Ironically, one of the reasons to have a close and loving relationship with your child is that it will be easier to punish her when you have to.

The main point here, and the first rule of effective punishment, is that any punishment must be *unpleasant* to be effective. If you want to punish a child by taking away something, for example, you have to take away something that the child will really miss, and you have to take it away for a long enough time to make your child long for it. If you want to punish a child by using a time-out, you have to make the time-out long enough so that the child feels bad about being isolated.

Most parents understand this general logic, but they don't punish effectively because they don't like making their child feel bad. The problem, though, is that punishment works only if your child feels bad enough when he's been punished to stop him from repeating the misbehavior the next time.

This is why you can't punish a child by sending him to a bedroom that is stocked with toys, video games, and more things to do for fun than you'd find on your average cruise ship. If your child doesn't mind being sent to his room, this cannot be used as an effective punishment. Similarly, it is of no value to put a child on a time-out and then take her off it the moment she complains about it.

I can't tell you how best to punish *your* child because for different children, different things cause them to feel bad. Trying to induce guilt in a child who wants to please you will be effective; the same technique will fail if your child doesn't really care about your opinion. Depriving a child of phone privileges will work for a highly social child with a lot of friends, but this same punishment will be ineffective with a child who is a quiet loner. Withholding a weekly allowance from a child who is dependent on you for money will work; withholding a weekly allowance from a teenager who has a part-time job will not.

You probably can figure out how best to punish your child in a way that is going to be meaningful. If you have more than one child, you may need to punish each one differently, depending on their age, personality, interests, and so forth.

There are two other elements to effective punishment to keep in mind.

The first will come as no surprise to you: To be effective, punishment has to be administered consistently. In fact, the consistency with which you punish your child's misbehavior is far more important than the way you do it. If you wish to stop your child from using foul language, punishing him each time he swears (for example, by deducting a portion of his weekly allowance for each offensive word) will get rid of the behavior faster than a more intermittent, less consistent approach. Punishment works only when your child can count on you to react in the same way to his misbehavior every single time.

The second element of effective punishment is the speed with which you do it. The quicker you punish a child after she's misbehaved, the more effective it is going to be. If you are trying to stop your child from whining, for example, it's best to punish her when she begins to whine rather than wait until her whining has really started to bother you. This is especially true with younger children, because the longer the delay between an infraction and a punishment, the more room there is for your child to be confused about what she's done that's wrong. If you wait until your child has whined for the tenth time before you punish her for it, she won't know whether what she did wrong was to whine, or to whine ten times. You'll regret that lack of clarity when she whines nine times on the next occasion.

When a child receives a tongue-lashing right after he has run out into the street, the punishment is much more likely to prevent similar actions in the future than if a parent delays lecturing the child until later in the day. Similarly, a parent who catches a child stealing and expresses disappointment at that moment is more likely to make an impression on the child than is a parent who temporarily ignores the misdeed and waits for some time before reacting. This is why "Wait until your father gets home" is not a very good disciplinary technique: It inserts too much time between the infraction and the punishment.

If you can't bear the thought of making your child feel bad, you are going to have to rely on using reward and explanation as your only disciplinary tools. That's certainly possible to do, but it will make your life difficult, because there are some situations in which punishment is the simplest and most effective response. When your child continues to hit his little brother despite your telling him not to, he ought to be punished. When your child steals something, he ought to be punished for it. When your child knowingly lies to you, he ought to be punished for it.

Whether you are a parent who uses punishment frequently or sparingly is less important than doing it correctly. It's pointless to punish your child halfway, and actually cruel to do so, because all you will have done is make your child feel bad, but not quite bad enough to have any lasting impact.

It is fine to punish your child when you need to, so long as the particular punishment you use is not physical, verbally abusive, or harsh in some other way. However, when you punish your child, make sure that the punishment is unpleasant, consistent, and swiftly applied.

If the idea of making your child feel bad by punishing her still bothers you, think about it this way: The more effectively you use punishment, the less you'll have to do it.

Never Use Physical Punishment

IF YOU HAD to choose between two equally effective medications, one of which has terrible side effects and one of which does not, I assume you'd choose the one without the bad side effects.

If you are choosing between two equally effective forms of punishment, I hope you will use the same logic. Two different types of punishment can be equivalent in their short-term effectiveness but have markedly different side effects.

Of all the forms of punishment that parents use, the one with the worst side effects is physical punishment. Physical punishment is no more effective than other types of punishment—in fact, in many situations it is *less* effective—and it has been proven to have a harmful effect on children's development. That's why you should never spank, hit, slap, or otherwise physically punish your child.

When I say *never*, I mean *never*. No matter how angry you are. No matter what your child has done. No matter how frustrated, annoyed, desperate, or fed up you are. In the long run, when you use physical punishment, you are creating more problems than you are solving.

The main side effect of physical punishment is excessive aggression. Children who are spanked, hit, or slapped are more prone to fighting with other children. They are more likely to be bullies and more likely to use aggression to solve disputes with others. Who can blame them? Their parents have taught them that hitting someone is an acceptable way to solve a problem.

Excessive aggression is a serious enough problem in its own right, but it also leads to other, equally serious difficulties. Children who are overly aggressive are more likely to be rejected by their classmates, to get into trouble in school, and to develop early conduct problems. All of these place a child at risk for academic difficulty, forming friendships with antisocial peers, and delinquency. Spanking your child will increase the likelihood of all of these problems.

I'm sure you know plenty of people who were spanked or hit as children but who nevertheless ended up as popular, successful, model citizens. (Maybe you or your spouse is one of them.) There are always individual exceptions to any general rule, but these cases don't prove that the rule is incorrect. As you know, not everyone who smokes develops lung cancer, but you'd be a fool to argue that this proves that smoking doesn't increase the risk of developing the disease. By the same token, not every child who has been physically punished develops aggressive behavior problems, but their risk for this is significantly higher than in other children's.

Physical punishment is also a poor choice because it can easily escalate out of control and cause a serious injury to the child. Few parents who hit their children actually intend to injure them. (Those who do need professional counseling.) But some parents have a difficult time controlling their anger once they start spanking; others simply do not know their own strength. If you regularly spank or hit your child, sooner or later she is going to get hurt.

Given that you have effective alternatives available, why take a chance with your child?

If you need to punish your child, do so by telling him that you're disappointed in how he has behaved, putting him on a time-out (if he is young), or depriving him of something he wants or enjoys (if he is older). These work just as well as physical punishment, but they do not have adverse side effects.

Let me repeat myself, just to make sure you get my point: Never spank, hit, slap, or otherwise physically punish your child. The link between physical punishment and children's aggression has been scientifically documented in hundreds, if not thousands, of research studies.

Physical punishment is bad for children.

Don't Be Verbally Abusive

I'VE SEEN SOME parents shout and scream at their child in a manner that is so harsh it borders on verbal abuse.

Like physical punishment, speaking to your child in an excessively angry or cruel way has side effects that over time will adversely affect his development. In fact, children who have been verbally abused by their parents often have more psychological problems than those who have been physically abused. For example, children whose parents are constantly nasty, insulting, or demeaning are at heightened risk for many types of difficulties, ranging from poor self-esteem to clinical depression.

Being firm does not require being mean. They are two completely different things.

When you are disciplining your child for misbehavior, there is no need for name-calling ("You're such a baby"), sarcasm ("That was a really bright idea"), humiliation ("I can't believe I've raised such a rotten child"), or accusation ("You're always making my life miserable"). It's not necessary to berate your child, shout at her, or drive her to tears over what she did for her to get your point. She will get the point just as well, if not better, if you remain calm and composed.

It's not just that harsh verbal discipline has harmful side effects. It's also ineffective, for two reasons.

First, your success as a parent depends in part on the degree to which your child believes that you have his best interests at heart. If you constantly tell your child how much you dislike him, how incompetent he is, or how you wish he were more like someone else (a sibling, a cousin, his best friend), you will undermine the quality of the emotional relationship the two of you have, and that will make you a less effective parent. Remember, telling your child that you are disappointed in what he has done (which is fine to do) will work as a punishment only if your child cares about your opinion of him. The meaner and nastier you are, though, the less your child will care what you think. It's common sense.

Second, when the content of what you are saying to your child is hostile or is delivered in an especially angry way, your child's attention will be drawn to the tone of the message rather than to the real substance of what you are trying to get across. Have you ever accidentally cut someone off while driving and had the person swear at you and make an obscene gesture? As soon as that happens, your mind drifts from what *you* did ("I really should have looked in my rearview mirror before changing lanes") to what the other driver is doing ("Imagine the nerve of that guy!"). When someone screams at us, we often become so emotionally aroused that we can't pay full attention to the content of what's being said. The same is true for your child when you scream and shout.

When you are talking to your child about his misbehavior, you want him to focus on the message, not the way it's being delivered. When he walks away from the conversation, you want his mind to be on what he did and why he shouldn't do it again, not on the fact that you screamed at him. That's hard for him to do if you've been ranting and raving.

I'm not saying that you should treat misbehavior casually. But you can deliver a strong and meaningful message ("You are not to draw on the wall with crayons") in a calm but firm tone of voice. If you want to raise your voice for emphasis, just don't overdo it. A little anger goes a long way.

One good way to avoid harsh verbal discipline is to focus your remarks on your child's behavior rather than on your child. There is a world of difference between saying "I can't stand what you did" and saying "I can't stand you," and between saying "That was a terrible thing to do" and saying "You are a terrible child." In each case, the first statement makes a child feel bad about what he did; the second makes him feel bad about who he is. You want to accomplish the former without inadvertently doing the latter.

A second point is to focus on the specific behavior in question rather than make sweeping generalizations. Most of the nasty or mean things that parents say to their child are broad swipes at his competence ("You can't do anything right"), personality ("You've always been a difficult child"), morals ("You're a liar"), or future potential ("You're never going to amount to anything"). When you are responding to your child's misbehavior, limit what you say to the situation at hand ("This was the wrong thing to do." "Don't lie to me about this." "You are being very difficult when you do this." "Behaving this way is going to get you into trouble in the future."). You'll find that fewer harsh sentiments come out when you are talking more specifically.

Finally, think about what you say before you say it. Most of the time, when parents are excessively harsh, it's because they've reacted quickly and in anger. When you are disciplining your child about something that's just happened, take a deep breath before you speak and choose your words deliberately. Be mindful about what you say and how you say it.

One of the most important things you have going for you as a parent is that your child comes into the world with a natural desire to please you. When you use harsh discipline, whether it is verbal or physical, you gradually erode this inclination.

You may get away with harsh verbal discipline when your child is little, but by the time he has turned eight or nine, you will have cashed in all of your emotional chips. You can't afford to do that. You've still got a lot of child rearing ahead of you.

Controlling Your Anger

NEVER DISCIPLINE your child when you are angry. It only increases the chance that you will be excessively harsh, either physically or verbally.

There will inevitably be times when you are absolutely furious with your child. When he does not cooperate and you are in a hurry to get somewhere. When you have a pounding headache and he won't stop nagging you. When she has ruined something that you really care about. When he has spoken to you in an extremely nasty or disrespectful way. When you discover that she has been lying to you all along about something you've discussed several times.

In any close relationship, whether it is between relatives, spouses, friends, or parents and children, there are bound to be conflicts, arguments, and frustrations that leave one or both people angry. It is perfectly normal to feel angry at your child from time to time. This doesn't mean that you're a bad parent, that you have a bad child, or that you have a bad relationship.

There is a big difference, though, between feeling angry at someone and letting that person have it. I'm sure you've been in plenty of situations where what you really wanted to do was scream, swear, or slap someone—but you didn't. So you know that you can control your anger when you must. (If you can't, you need to learn how. Uncontrollable anger may be entertaining to watch in a movie, but in real life, it's not a winning trait.) Control your anger when you are disciplining your child. Make yourself do it.

I've said elsewhere that punishment is most effective when it is applied immediately. How can you do this, then, when your child has done something that has really made you angry?

When you feel yourself getting angry with your child over something he's done, take a deep breath, count to three, and tell your child in a firm but measured tone that you are furious. Then wait until you've calmed down to actually do something about the situation. Explain why you are punishing your child, and then punish him.

With a child who is seven or older, you can also say something like "I'm so mad at what you did that I can't even discuss it right now. But we are going to talk about this later."

Make sure, though, that you actually *do* something once you've settled down (for example, deprive your child of something she likes or force her to do a chore that she detests). You want your child to associate your anger over her misbehavior with a genuinely unpleasant consequence. But you don't want that consequence to be a slap on the behind or a verbal assault. As I've explained, physical punishment and verbal abuse have harmful side effects.

The time that elapses between your telling your child that you are furious and the point at which you actually take action should be only as long as it takes you to calm down. Don't draw it out any longer than you need to. Remember, you want to punish your child as close in time to the misbehavior as possible, because a swift response is more effective than a delayed response.

I know you've probably been told that it's important for children to feel comfortable with their emotions, whether they are positive or negative. I agree that children should grow up feeling that anger, just like happiness and sadness, is a normal human feeling. And you may ask yourself if your excessively controlled expression of anger will stifle your child's emotional development.

The answer is no, it won't. There is no evidence that children who are exposed to open displays of parental anger are emotionally healthier than their peers, and plenty of proof that just the opposite is true. Children whose parents yell at them often are more likely to feel anxious and fearful and to have trouble controlling their own anger in their relationships with others.

Although it's great for children to feel comfortable with their emotions, it's also important that they learn to express them in ways that are socially appropriate. Hitting, yelling, and screaming are rarely effective ways of expressing anger or frustration. It's important to help your child learn that he can feel angry and express his anger without losing control of himself or the situation.

If you are accustomed to disciplining your child when you are angry, following my advice about pausing before you act will feel oddly forced at first. Once you've tried it for a while, it will start to feel more natural.

Cut down on the yelling and screaming. Your child's behavior will improve right alongside yours.

The Right Way to Punish

NOW THAT YOU KNOW what makes punishment effective—it needs to be unpleasant, consistent, and swiftly administered, and it should not be harsh—we can talk about how you should actually do it.

Effective punishment needs to include five elements, usually in the following order:

- An *identification* of the specific act that was wrong.
- A statement describing the *impact* of the misbehavior.
- A suggestion for one or more *alternatives* to the undesirable behavior.
- A clear statement of what the *punishment* is going to be.
- A statement of your *expectation* that your child will do better the next time.

Try to do all five of these whenever you punish your child.

Your four-year-old has been told that she should not whine when she can't have her way. Now she's whining because you won't let her have a cookie right before dinner. Say something like this: "Please don't whine when you want something (Identification). It puts me in a bad mood (Impact). If you are hungry and it is nearly dinner time, you can have a carrot or a piece of celery (Alternative). I'm going to put you on a time-out until you've settled down (Punishment). I know the next time I say you can't have something, you won't whine about it (Expectation)."

By the way, a good rule of thumb is that a time-out should last about one minute for each year of your child's age (that is, four minutes for a four-year-old). When you put your child on a time-out, make her sit by herself in a place where there is nothing for her to do but sit there. (Don't put her on a time-out in a room where she has things to play with.) Ignore her during the time-out, even if she complains, and go about your business. If she gets up before the time-out is over, tell her firmly to return to where she was sitting, that you are making the time-out longer because she got up, and add thirty additional seconds to the amount of remaining time.

Your six-year-old has been told not to color with markers while sitting on the living room couch, but you see your child doing this anyway. Say something like this: "I've asked you not to color with your markers while you are sitting on this couch (Identification). These markers leave stains that are very hard to clean (Impact). When you want to color, please do it at the kitchen table (Alternative). Please give me your markers. You are not allowed to use them for a week (Punishment). I know you probably just forgot this time, but it's important that you remember next time (Expectation)."

When it is possible, link the punishment to the infraction. Taking away a toy that a child has misused for a period of time is a good way to reinforce the rule.

Your nine-year-old has tracked mud all over the kitchen floor, even though you have repeatedly asked him to make sure his shoes are clean before he comes in from playing outside. "I've told you lots of times that you need to wipe your shoes so that you don't track mud all over the house (Identification). I just cleaned the floor, and now it needs to be cleaned again (Impact). There's a mat outside the back door. If you can't get the dirt off by wiping your shoes on the mat, just take your shoes off and leave them outside (Alternative). Now, please get a mop and clean the floor (Punishment). You're usually so good about everything—please try to remember the next time (Expectation)."

Having a child undo damage that he's done is an effective punishment as long as the task is onerous enough to make him regret his infraction.

Your thirteen-year-old has told you that she spends her afternoons at the house of a friend whose mother is home, but you discover that the mother is never there. You are furious that she's been lying to you. Say something like this: "You told me that Susan's mother is always home when you go over there. You know that you are allowed to go over to a friend's house only if an adult is present (Identification). If I don't know where you are after school, it makes it very hard for me to concentrate at work (Impact). If you want to do something after school other than what we've agreed on, I want you to call me at work and ask permission first (Alternative). Right now, I'm too angry with you to discuss this, but I do want to talk about the fact that you lied to me. Please go to your room, and I will be there in a few minutes. [After a few minutes]. I've decided to ground you for a week, starting today. That means coming straight home after school every day and staying home every evening and over the entire weekend (Punishment). You've rarely lied to me before. From now on, I expect you to tell me the truth (Expectation)."

Remember, never discipline your child when you are angry.

Your sixteen-year-old, who has a learner's permit, has taken the family car for a drive without your knowledge, even though he has no license. He's one week away from taking his driver's test. "It's against the law for you to be driving without an older, licensed driver in the car with you. You may already know how to drive, but until you've passed your driver's test, you are not allowed to drive on your own (Identification). You and I both can get into a lot of trouble for this (Impact). If you need to go somewhere and I am not around, ask someone who has a license to come and pick you up (Alternative). Because you've done this, I'm not permitting you to take your driver's test for another month (Punishment). I'm sure you understand why obeying the law has to be the rule around here (Expectation)."

Again, when possible, link the punishment (delaying the driver's test) to the offense (driving without a license).

Whenever you need to punish your child, try to follow this general outline: Identify the infraction, describe its impact, suggest an alternative, describe the punishment, and say you expect better behavior the next time.

That's the right way to punish.

Explain Your Rules and Decisions

Be Clear About What You Expect

Reasoning with Your Child

"Because I Said So"

Hear Your Child's Point of View

Admit Your Mistakes

Be Clear About What You Expect

GOOD PARENTS have expectations that they want their child to live up to.

In order for your child to do this, your expectations have to be clear, and they have to be appropriate. If they aren't crystal clear, there's a good possibility that your child will be doing what she *thinks* you expect, but disappointing you just the same. That's a recipe for conflict. And if your expectations aren't appropriate, your child will constantly try for unattainable goals. That's a recipe for disappointment and hurt feelings.

Sometimes, parents' expectations are not clear because they're left unstated rather than made explicit. You just assume your child knows what you expect from him. You assume he knows that he's not supposed to leave wet towels on his bed. You assume he knows that he's supposed to call you when he's going to be late for dinner. You assume he knows that he needs to walk the dog as soon as he gets home from school rather than waiting until after he's fixed himself a snack and played a couple of video games. You assume that when he sees you shoveling snow off the front walk or weeding the garden, he knows that he's to come out and lend a hand.

Not only is your child not a psychic, he's also not an adult. What is obvious to you may not be evident to a twelve-year-old. He doesn't have the priorities, judgment, or experience that you have.

Don't assume that something that is so obvious to you that it goes without saying will also be clear to him. Make sure you say what you have in mind. You'll be surprised how much of what you've taken for granted is news to him. You may think that something is just common sense or common courtesy, but what's common among adults is often rare among children.

Sometimes parents' expectations aren't clear because they're stated too vaguely. It's not enough to tell your ten-year-old that you expect her to keep her room clean, practice the piano, read before she goes to bed, or help out around the house. You have in mind a whole list of specifics that these directives imply, but your child may not know exactly what they are. She may think that cleaning up her room means putting her CDs back on her bookshelf. You need to explain that cleaning her room includes this, but that it also includes putting clothes away if they're clean and in the hamper if not, straightening up her desk, dusting off her dresser, and vacuuming once a week. She may think that fifteen minutes of daily piano practice suffices, whereas you have three times that amount in mind. She thinks that thumbing through this week's *People* magazine is reading before bed, but what you really expect is that she'll spend an hour with a challenging novel. When you say "help out around the house," you have one thing in mind, but her understanding is entirely different.

Children of all ages, even when they have reached adolescence, need a lot of specific direction. When you tell your child what you expect, make sure you spell it out in detail. If your child is young and your expectation has multiple components (such as cleaning up a bedroom), it doesn't hurt to make a checklist for your child to follow, at least until she's gotten the hang of it. If it is possible to use a specific number when describing an expectation—the time your teenager is supposed to be home from a concert, the number of minutes you expect her to practice her instrument—use one. That will prevent a lot of misunderstanding.

Another reason your expectations may not be clear to your child is that they're not entirely clear to you. If you're not sure what you expect from your child, there is no way he can possibly know what you want.

When you agreed to get a puppy, you told your nine-year-old that you expected him to help take care of the pet, but have you thought through what you really meant by this? Are you expecting him to walk the dog every day or once a week? Are you envisioning that he will be responsible for making sure the dog's water bowl is full? For bathing him every month?

When you decided to go back to work, you explained to your thirteen-year-old that he was going to have to pitch in and do more around the house. But have you given any thought to what exactly you expect from him?

When your teenager asked if she could take on a part-time job to earn extra pocket money, you told her that she could work, but only if she did well enough in school. But what does "well enough" really mean to you? Trying her hardest? Earning straight As? Doing better than her classmates? Doing better than she did last year? All of these examples could be construed as indicators of doing "well enough." If you're not sure, your child can't possibly be.

Before you communicate an expectation to your child, make sure you're clear about it yourself. If you're married, talk it over with your spouse so that it's clear to everyone.

It's important that your expectations be clear, and it's also important that they are appropriate for someone your child's age. Tailor your expectations to match your child's maturity level. Your expectations should be set so that meeting them requires a level of maturity that slightly exceeds what your child has shown up to that point, but that is still within your child's reach. If they aren't, you're only going to frustrate your child.

Psychologists use the term "scaffolding" to describe this process, in which you set up a situation for your child that she can successfully accomplish, at the same time permitting her to move beyond where she had been previously.

Suppose you believe that your child is now old enough to stay home alone for a period of time without needing a babysitter. (There isn't a magic age for this, by the way. A lot depends on the safety of your community, whether there are neighbors nearby, how fearful your child is, and so on.) Instead of having her first experience with this occur on a Saturday night when you and your spouse are going out to dinner and a movie, try this during the day, while you are at a neighbor's house for a half-hour chat over a cup of coffee. Even the most confident child is bound to feel a little nervous the first time she is left alone, but being left alone during the day for a half hour while you are next door is far less anxiety-provoking than spending a whole evening at home after dark while you are a twenty-minute drive away. (Many times, a child who is nervous about being left alone won't let on, because she wants to appear mature, so it's best to phase this sort of thing in gradually regardless of what your child tells you.) If your child handles the short time alone well, the next time you can leave her alone for a slightly longer period and gradually increase your expectations with each successive opportunity.

By the same token, there will be times when your child is not able to meet your expectations. Perhaps you thought your child could wash the car on his own and you discover that he didn't really do a thorough job. You may have overestimated his maturity or expected him to do something that is beyond what a child his age is capable of. If this is the case, avoid turning the situation into a failure experience for him, and don't dwell on what went wrong. Focus instead on what went right and help him figure out what he might have done differently or better. If you think he can master the situation on another try, give him some instruction and a second chance. If you don't think this is possible, set your expectations a bit lower.

In other words, create expectations that help your child demonstrate just how mature he is. Set him up to succeed.

Reasoning with Your Child

IT'S ALWAYS BEST to explain the reasoning behind any rule you set, because children are more likely to comply if they agree that a rule is necessary and fair.

Whether an explanation alone is enough to get your child to comply is a different matter. For many children it is. For other children, you may have to accompany the explanation with some form of punishment for refusing to obey you or with a reward for complying. However, alone or in combination with another disciplinary strategy, explaining your rules and decisions is important.

Most parents end up explaining a lot of things, whether they like it or not, because children invariably begin asking "Why?" as soon as they are old enough to question things. Many parents don't tailor their explanation to match the intellectual level of their child. Generally, parents overexplain to young children and underexplain to adolescents.

There's no need to reason with your three-year-old as if she has the logical capabilities of a teenager. By the same token, you can't expect an adolescent to accept the sort of reasoning that would satisfy a preschooler.

To choose the right approach to reasoning with children of different ages, you need to have some appreciation of how children's thinking develops. Young children, elementary-school-age children, and teenagers don't think about rules in the same way. Here's a good general guideline:

- For children under six, your explanation needs to be reasonable.
- For children between six and eleven, your explanation needs to be reasonable and logical.
- For children older than eleven, your explanation needs to be reasonable, logical, and consistent with other things you have said or done.

When they are younger than six, children don't question the logical basis of rules. They may ask why they have to comply with them, but what they are really asking is *whether* they have to comply, not what your reasoning is. For children of this age, almost any explanation for a rule will do, as long as it sounds reasonable and is honest. (I don't like to see parents lie to their children, even if the lies are harmless. It sends the message that it's okay to fib when you need to.)

Your five-year-old asks why he needs to pick up his toys. Tell him it's because you are worried that someone will trip over them and fall, or because you need to vacuum the floor, or because you don't want any of them to get lost. Or tell him that you are tired from picking up things and need him to do this to help you, or that you are worried that the dog will damage them, or that you don't like the house to look messy. As I said, almost any explanation that is reasonable will suffice. (For that matter, "Because I said so" will also work if your child is young enough, but, as I explain in the next section, that's the one response to "Why?" that you should try to avoid.)

There is really no point in trying to help a child who is younger than six understand the "underlying principle" of one of your rules, because he doesn't have the intellectual skills necessary to comprehend at this level. When reasoning with a child who is this age, keep it simple and keep it concrete.

For example, if you want your four-year-old to eat her carrots and she asks why, don't launch into a long-winded explanation of the food pyramid and where vegetables are categorized on it. It is better to say that carrots are good for her than to try to explain what a balanced diet is and why it is important. She won't be able to make the logical leap from "It's good to follow a balanced diet" to "Therefore, I should eat my carrots," because this requires being able to take a general principle and apply it to a specific case, which is difficult, if not impossible, for young children to do. It's fine to teach your child about the importance of eating fruits and vegetables or about foods that are healthy and those that are not, but this is a separate issue from getting her to eat her carrots when you are at the dinner table. Don't waste your time with elaborate scientific explanations when a simple and straightforward one will do. Save the dissertation on vitamins and their importance to the immune system until she is older.

Between the ages of six and eleven, children develop the ability to use logic, but they still have problems reasoning with abstractions. To them, rules need to be reasonable and sensible, but they should be specific. Examples of explanations that work fine at this age include: "In our family, we don't use swear words because they are rude"; "Everyone has to pitch in and do some chores, because there is too much work for me to do alone"; and "Getting your homework done is more important than watching television."

You can expect a child of this age to understand the logic

behind your rules, but don't expect him to spontaneously extend the general principles they are based on to new situations. For example, when you explain to your nine-year-old that you don't want him to throw wet clothes under his bed because mildew grows in a dark, wet environment, he will understand this, and, with a few reminders, he will probably remember to follow this rule. But the same child who now understands why he shouldn't throw wet clothes under his bed is still likely to place wet towels in a hamper, even though this violates the same principle. His thinking is more sophisticated than it had been when he was younger, but it is still concrete in many respects.

What this means on a more practical level is that when you are disciplining a child who is between six and eleven, explain the specific logic behind specific rules. If your six-year-old asks why she has to wear a seat belt, say "Because this helps keep you from slamming forward into the seat in front of you in case someone accidentally hits our car or I have to stop short." (A four-year-old would be satisfied with just being told that the seat belt helps to keep her safe.) If your nine-year-old asks why he needs to straighten up his room, you might say "Because the floor can't be vacuumed with your clothes all strewn about, and it is unhealthy for all that dust and dirt to accumulate." (With a younger child, only the first half of the explanation would be necessary, but now that your child is nine, your logic needs to be spelled out.) If your eleven-year-old asks why he needs to be in bed by ten o'clock, you might say "Because that's the only way you will get enough sleep, and if you are tired in the morning, you will have a hard time concentrating in school." (Again, with a younger child, the first half of the explanation will suffice.)

A child who is twelve or older will have the same, or nearly the same, logic skills that you do. This is the age during which children often become argumentative, because they are looking for the flaws, gaps, and inconsistencies in other people's logic, including their parents'. For an explanation to be successful at this age, it must not only be reasonable and sensible, but its underlying logic has to be consistent with other rules that you have, other things that you've said, and other things that you've done. Otherwise, you're going to be challenged.

If your fourteen-year-old wants to know why she can't wear a tight-fitting, low-cut blouse to school, you might say "Dressing in a sexually provocative way is inappropriate in school, where people should be concentrating on their classes, not on each other's bodies. When you dress this way, it sends a message to your teachers that you are more interested in boys than in school, and that's the wrong message to send." (However, if *you* dress in provocative clothes when you go to the office, your explanation may be unconvincing.) If your sixteen-year-old wants to know why he can't have his own car, you might say "The expense involved in getting another car isn't just in the purchase of the car—we've got to insure it and maintain it as well. We're trying to save money for college now and need to cut out all unnecessary expenses." (Of course, if you are spending money on other frivolous things, your teenager will be the first one to point this out to you, which is why your explanation needs to be consistent with your other behavior.)

To reason with your child in an appropriate way, you have to have a good understanding of how someone your child's age thinks. Very young children see the world in absolutes; to them, something is right because a person of authority has said so. Elementary school children are swayed by logic; to them, a rule is right because it makes sense. Teenagers respond well to rules that are based on clear and consistent principles; to them, a rule is right because it serves some higher purpose.

If you keep this framework in mind and adapt your reasoning to fit your child's stage of development, your explanations will carry a lot more weight.

"Because I Said So"

MOST PARENTS promise themselves that they will never say "Because I said so" to their child, but almost all of them break this promise at some time. It gets tiring to have to provide explanation after explanation to your child every time you ask him to do something.

If your instincts tell you that "Because I said so" is not the right way to answer your child's request for a rationale, follow them. You're absolutely correct.

When your child asks you why she should do something you've asked her to do, she may be complaining about your demand, but she may also be asking a question about the way the world works. (Sometimes it's more the first than the second, and sometimes the reverse is true.) When you pour your child a glass of milk with her dinner and she asks why she is not allowed to have a soft drink, she is not only stating that a soft drink is what she'd prefer, but she is also asking a perfectly reasonable question about why one drink is preferable to the other. If you can answer it, you should.

"Because I said so" tells your child that you don't have a good reason for your request. You may feel that parents don't need to have reasons for the things they ask of their children, and you're certainly entitled to your own opinion about that. But once your child starts to ask questions about the world around him, you should to try to answer them as best you can. "Because I said so" is not informative, and it's not going to satisfy an inquisitive, curious child once he's turned four or five.

To me, the most important reason to avoid using "Because I said so" as a means of gaining your child's compliance is that you want your child to get into the habit of asking other people to provide rationales for requests she is unsure or unhappy about. When you say "Because I said so," you are, in essence, saying "Because I have more power than you and I can make you do it." This might be fine so long as the more forceful person your child is questioning is a parent who has his best interests in mind. But suppose it's someone else? When a more forceful playmate suggests that your six-year-old should jump off a ten-foot-tall jungle gym onto the pavement, should your child comply just because his friend says so? When a teacher mistakenly gives your twelve-year-old a lower grade than she deserves, should she accept it because her teacher says so? When your fifteen-year-old's boyfriend asks her to sleep with him, would you want her to agree just because he says so?

When your child asks for a reason to comply with a request you've made, provide one that makes sense and is phrased in a way that is appropriate for your child's age. It takes more time in the short run to do this than to reflexively say "Because I said so," but in the long run your child will be more likely to mind you if he understands what you're trying to accomplish. If you provide a reasonable explanation for something today ("Soft drinks are bad for your teeth, and it's not good to have them very often"), it's less likely that your child will challenge you on this same issue tomorrow. (Why should he, if the answer is going to be the same?) When you use "Because I said so," however, your child may think that your answer is merely a function of your mood and may challenge you again when he thinks you're in a better mood and more likely to give in.

If you really can't think of a reasonable explanation to give your child, perhaps your request is just for your own convenience. That's fine. Just say something like "Because it will make me happy" or "Because it makes my day easier."

If your request has no good reason other than to show your child that you are the boss, your request is a bad one. Your authority over your child should be grounded in your experience, your knowledge, and your judgment, not in your power. Your child should respect you because you are the parent, but obey you because you are correct.

Forcing your child to comply with your requests without providing a justification for them is going to foster dependence, conformity, and susceptibility to peer pressure. If you don't want your child to get into the habit of doing things because someone "says so," you need to break the "Because I said so" habit.

Don't do it because I said so. Do it because it is the sensible thing to do.

Hear Your Child's Point of View

YOU ARE NOT the only one who has an opinion about the rules that structure your child's life. Your child has a point of view, too. It's often a good idea to find out what it is.

Sometimes, your child's opinion is reasonable, sensible, and logical. Many times, it is not. But you'll never know if you never ask.

More important than whether your child is right or wrong, soliciting your child's opinion tells her that you value her point of view and are willing to look at things from her perspective. This does a number of things that will make your job as a parent easier and help your child develop her intellectual skills.

First, when you make a good-faith effort to understand your child's point of view, you convey the idea that your decision making is based on what makes sense and not simply on your opinion. After all, the reason we ask someone else's opinion—at least when we do so authentically—is to see if our opinion is shared by others and, if not, whether our point of view should be amended. Asking your child what he thinks says that you're open to other points of view, and that shows that you are reasonable. Remember, your child is much more likely to abide by your rules if he thinks they make sense.

Second, when you solicit your child's opinion, you make her a part of the decision-making process. This is good in general and especially important in instances where you and your child disagree. It turns out that when decisions go against us—when, for example, you lose an appeal to have a speeding ticket overturned, fail in an effort to convince a teacher to change your grade on a paper, or are unsuccessful in persuading a salesperson to take back something you'd like to return—the worst thing is to feel that your point of view was given short shrift. When we feel that we didn't have a chance to explain our side of things, we usually are more annoyed with the outcome, even if the outcome is no different than it would have been had we had a chance to plead our case. There is something about walking away from a situation feeling that you gave it your best shot that makes it easier to accept that you didn't get your way. Your child is no different. When you and she disagree, give her a chance to give it her best shot. She'll sulk less.

Third, hearing what your child has to say will help you understand how she looks at things, and this will make your job as a parent easier. Let me give you an example of what I mean.

Your twelve-year-old appears at the breakfast table one weekday morning with thickly applied eyeliner, mascara, and lipstick—made up in a way you think is absolutely inappropriate for school. Without giving her a chance to make her case, you immediately send her back upstairs and order her to remove her makeup. Although she starts to say "But," you cut her off and say that there is no discussing the matter. She bursts out of the room in tears, and minutes later you hear her slam the bathroom door shut behind her. This is not what you need before heading to the office.

Suppose, instead, you had been willing to let her finish her sentence, and discovered that the reason she's made up is that all of her close friends have been wearing cosmetics to school and have been teasing her because she hasn't. Cast in this light, her desire to wear makeup to school now seems more reasonable: She's trying to fit in, which is normal behavior for a twelve-year-old girl. You realize that the real issue isn't the specific makeup she's wearing, but whether she can wear any makeup to school at all. Although you might still insist that she take off the excessive makeup she had been wearing, you might not have overreacted when she appeared at the table had you given her a chance to explain. Perhaps you and she both could live with her going off to school with a more understated look.

There is often much to learn by hearing what your child has to say on the subject. Letting him express his point of view, and even actively soliciting it when he doesn't do so spontaneously, allows you to be a more sympathetic parent. As I've said, part of what goes into being a good parent is being able to get inside the mind of someone your child's age. Finding out what and how your child thinks about the rules you have is an important way of achieving this.

Discussions between you and your child about rules and expectations not only permit you to understand how she thinks, they also help *her* understand how *you* think. This will make it easier for her to anticipate what you want without your having to ask all the time. If she has a general idea of what's important to you, she doesn't have to read your mind. If she knows, for example, that the reason you expect her to wash the dishes after dinner is that you think it's important for family members to share household responsibilities, she's more likely to volunteer to help you rake leaves or clean out the basement.

Finally, discussions about rules are an important arena in which your child hones his abilities to reason and formulate a persuasive argument. You may think of arguments with your child as debates about the specific issue at hand, and of course they are. But they are also more than this. They are opportunities for your child to make his position known to someone who is smarter and more powerful. He's going to be in this position plenty of times in the future, and it's good to let him practice this with you.

I think it's a good idea for parents to solicit their child's opinion about rules, routines, and expectations from time to time, in addition to being willing to listen when their child brings up the subject. I'm not suggesting that each time you explain yourself you ask your child to weigh in—this will be tiresome for both you and your child, especially when you are just doing so for the sake of seeming like an understanding parent (your child will see through this sooner or later, anyway). But if the issue is clearly one that your child is upset about (you've refused to increase your thirteen-year-old's allowance; she says hers is much less than any of her friends') or one that you yourself are not entirely sure about (your sixteen-year-old announces that she'd like to start a part-time job during the school year), ask your child what she thinks.

It may be an inconvenient irritant that your child has his own opinions about matters you believe are a parent's business, but this is a small price to pay for having a child who won't be shy about asserting his opinion in other situations when he doesn't think he's getting a fair shake. Remember, the lessons your child learns in his relationship with you are going to shape the way he behaves when he is with other people. You can't raise a child who will roll over at home but speak his mind when he is with his friends.

Admit Your Mistakes

IT DOESN'T MAKE any sense for you to stick to a rule whose logic your child can poke holes through. Standing firm when you have no good reason to doesn't enhance your authority as a parent—it diminishes it.

I've never understood parents who won't admit to their children that they've been wrong about something. Acknowledging one's errors or misjudgments is a sign of maturity—a capacity you want to encourage in your child. If you behave stubbornly as a parent, it's hard to see why your child should behave any differently. Children learn as much, if not more, by watching their parents than by listening to them.

One reason parents are reluctant to admit their mistakes to their children is that they worry that once their child figures out they are wrong about *something*, he will start to think that they are wrong about *everything*. This is partially true, in that once your child figures out that you are wrong about something, it will suddenly dawn on him that it is possible for people to be parents and to still make mistakes. Realizing this will likely prompt him to question your judgment more than he had in the past, but questioning your judgment isn't the same as rejecting it. Besides, he is going to figure out sooner or later that you aren't perfect as a part of his normal intellectual development. Your admitting your mistakes has nothing to do with his change of opinion. (In fact, during early adolescence, he may even go through a temporary stage when his conviction that you are *always* wrong is just as irrationally unshakable as was his belief in your infallibility when he was a preschooler.) Given the fact that your child will eventually know that you aren't perfect, it's better that he sees you as fallible and candid, rather than fallible and deceitful.

It's a good idea for parents to step up and admit their mistakes once they realize that they have erred rather than waiting for their child to point them out first. If you change your opinion about your child's best friend, now that you've gotten to know her a bit, tell your child that you realize you had misjudged her. If you discover that a television show you had banned from your home is really not inappropriate after all, tell your child that you had a chance to watch it and have changed your mind. If you realize that you unfairly accused your child of something he hadn't done, apologize as soon as you can. If, after the fact, you conclude that the way you punished your child for a misdeed was excessively harsh, tell your child that you made a mistake and undo what you did.

Admitting when you've made a mistake that has had a direct impact on your child is one thing; telling your child about other mistakes you've made (in your marriage, at the office, when you were younger) is something entirely different. Parents understandably wonder how to handle mistakes they've made in the past or that their child simply is unaware of. Unfortunately, there is no easy or automatic answer to this; it really depends on what the mistake was, your child's age, and how intimate your relationship is with your child.

If what you did conflicts with what you are trying to teach your child (you smoked cigarettes when you were eleven, and you've always told your eleven-year-old that it is wrong to smoke), your child will have a hard time reconciling things until she is twelve or so, and even then she may feel as if your current stance is hypocritical. It may be worth shading the truth a bit so as not to confuse her ("I once took a puff, but it made me sick"). Once your child has reached adolescence, she'll have the cognitive capability to understand that it is not unreasonable for you to now oppose something that you did when you were younger. She may accuse you of hypocrisy anyway, in which case your answer should be that your view of life has changed since you've become a parent. It's fine to say that you made mistakes when you were her age.

In general, I don't believe there is any reason to spontaneously disclose mistakes from your past, but you should acknowledge them if you've been asked directly by your child. Even then, you'll have to use your best judgment about how to answer your child's inquiry. The younger your child is and the more serious your transgression was, the more important it is to be discreet or avoid answering the question. An eight-year-old can't understand why someone would have smoked marijuana if it is against the law, and her questions about your past drug use might be best handled with white lies at this age ("It was so long ago that I really can't remember." "Even when I was young, I always thought it was important to obey the law."). In contrast, a fifteen-year-old who has just watched a documentary on the 1960s will be able to put the same behavior in context, and your answer to the same question might be different ("Yes, it was a time when people did a lot of foolish things." "Yes, but I stopped as soon as I left college."). And remember, when your child is young, it is fine to say that this is something you'd prefer to talk about when he is older.

As a general rule, I am not in favor of parents lying to their adolescent children, but there is an important difference between disclosing the gory details of one's past and letting your child know that you haven't led a perfect life. I suppose the main consideration is whether your child will profit in some way from what you have to say. Sharing a story from your past to teach your child a lesson (explaining how cheating on your chemistry final led to your failing the class) is potentially valuable, but bragging about illegal or unethical behavior whose consequences you were lucky to avoid is not. (Like it or not, you are a role model for your child.) When your child asks you if you had sex with anyone before you were married, saying that you were not a virgin when you got married is different from saying that you slept with more college classmates than you can remember. (And saying that someone's sex life is a private matter is a perfectly fine response, too.) When your child asks if you used illegal drugs when you were younger, saying that you experimented and decided that it wasn't for you is better than regaling your child with stories about your drug-related exploits.

Some parents erroneously believe that it is important for children to see them as infallible. It is true that very young children—those under six—tend to think that their parents don't make mistakes, but this doesn't mean that this is a desirable belief for them to have, or that it is one that we want them to hold on to when they are older. Young children believe many things that are immature and incorrect—that, for example, the sun sets in order to let people sleep, or that the tooth fairy replaces baby teeth with money—but they shed these beliefs as they get older and smarter. Like her belief in the tooth fairy, your child's need to see you as infallible will naturally fade as she ages. It's fine if you want to bask in your child's idealized view of you while it's still there, but please let her outgrow it.

When you are wrong, be the bigger person.

Treat Your Child with Respect

Getting and Giving Respect

Have Two-Way Conversations

"Don't Talk Back"

Let Your Child Act His Age

Children Treat Others the Way Their Parents
Treat Them

Getting and Giving Respect

Many parents worry too much about whether their child respects them, and they don't think enough about whether they
treat their child with respect. I know that this sentiment is not
going to sit well with parents who are especially hung up about
maintaining their authority, but please give me a chance to explain what I mean.

Children come into the world predisposed toward looking up
to their parents and wanting to be like them. As children get
older and see their parents' flaws, the parental rose loses some of
its bloom. This is natural, understandable, and, in many ways,

desirable. (After all, you want your child to have an honest view of the world, and that necessarily includes an honest view of you.) But if you treat your child kindly and fairly, are genuinely concerned about her well-being, and are a reasonably good role model, she will respect you, even as she develops a more accurate and objective impression of who you are and even if she disagrees with you and occasionally even goes against your wishes.

Even during times when your child is contrary, rebellious, or argumentative, he's probably not behaving this way out of disrespect. More likely, he's acting this way because he's going through a stage, like early adolescence, when challenging and contradicting you is a normal way of asserting his individuality. It's fine to insist that when your child disagrees with you, he express himself in a respectful manner, but if you try to force him to agree with you or keep his mouth shut "out of respect," you will only prolong the struggle. Respect is not measured in whether people agree with each other—it's measured in how they behave toward each other when they disagree.

I think it's important to give children the benefit of the doubt rather than to automatically assume that when they misbehave or argue they are going out of their way to behave disrespectfully or to make their parent's life difficult. Unless you have a lot of evidence to the contrary, you should assume that your child respects you and look elsewhere to interpret her behavior when she's acting in a way that is bothersome, contrary, disobedient, or frustrating. There is almost always a more reasonable explanation for a child's misbehavior than disrespect, spite, or deliberate oppositionalism, and if you look at your child's behavior in light of her particular stage of development, you'll usually be able to figure out what it is.

I'm not saying that you should accept your child's misbehavior—you shouldn't. Behavior that makes you feel as if your child does not respect you is rarely intended as a display of disrespect. If your child does something that makes you feel this way, the first question you should be asking is not "Why doesn't my child respect me?" or "How can I make my child respect me?" but "Why do I think my child did this?" *That* question will more likely lead to a productive solution to the problem, whatever it is.

So let's get beyond the question of whether your child respects you. Most likely, he does.

However, let me ask you this: Do you treat your child with respect?

By treating your child with respect, I don't mean treating him as if he were your equal when making decisions or turning your relationship into a friendship between peers. Neither of these things is good to do. You're the parent and he's the child.

There is a big difference between treating your child with respect and being his buddy. I'm always a little troubled when I hear a parent say "My child and I are best friends." If the parent and child feel very close, have mutual interests, and enjoy each other's company, that's fine. But your child's best friend should be someone close in age, because it is good for children's development to have at least one close friend with whom they can discuss experiences they are going through at the same time. It's one thing to tell your mother about a classmate you're head-over-heels in love with; it's something else entirely to share this experience with someone who is going through the same thing.

The other reason that you and your child should not be best friends—at least until your child is an adult—is that parents sometimes need to be able to assert their authority in ways that that can't be done with someone whom they otherwise treat as an equal. It is confusing to a child when his father is his best friend one day and a strict enforcer of rules the next. Along similar lines, behaving like a parent toward someone you have just treated as a close confidante is very difficult. It's fine for your child to understand that you're only human, but it's upsetting and oppressive to a child when he feels that his parents depend on him emotionally. You want your child's life to be as carefree as possible; don't burden him with your problems.

When I say that you should treat your child with respect, I mean you should give him the same courtesies you would give anyone else. Speak to him politely. Respect his opinion. Pay attention when he is speaking to you. Treat him kindly. Try to please him when you can. Don't worry—you can do all of these things and still maintain your authority as the parent. You can be friendly without being friends.

And then there are those parents for whom being friends with their child seems the last thing on their mind. They order their children around. They tell them to shut up. They say things that humiliate or embarrass them in front of other people. They berate them even after they've apologized for doing something wrong. They don't pay attention or feign interest when their chilren are talking. They interrupt them. They speak to others in front of them as if they did not exist.

You've known your child his entire life. The very least you can do is treat him as respectfully as you would treat someone you are meeting for the first time.

I'm not sure what is going on in the mind of a parent who is disrespectful toward his or her child. I suppose that, for some parents, treating their child in a bullying or impolite fashion is a way of demonstrating that they have the upper hand in the relationship. In their mind, if you can order someone around and that person cannot do the same in return, it confirms both to that person and to other observers that you are the more powerful member of the pair. On the other hand, they think, treating someone else respectfully raises doubts about which one of you is really in the driver's seat.

I don't think this view is accurate about life in general, and it certainly doesn't make sense as far as your relationship with your child is concerned. If you need to treat your child disrespectfully in order to clarify who's in charge, there are things you ought to be worrying about that are more important than whether your child respects you (such as why there is any doubt about who the authority is).

I'm sure you've observed plenty of people who treat those in positions of less power (employees, service providers, waiters, salespersons, and so on) with respect and others who are impolite and haughty. As you've probably come to realize, people who habitually treat less powerful persons badly neither earn those people's respect nor enhance their own image in the eyes of others. If anything, just the opposite is true. Moreover, beyond treating people respectfully because it is the right thing to do, anyone who knows anything about human nature knows that if your ultimate goal is to get someone to perform better, work harder, or provide better service, treating that person with respect is a far more successful strategy in the long run than making the person feel as if he is an underling.

The same basic principles apply where parents and their children are concerned. Treating your child with respect is not only the right thing to do, it is the smart thing to do. Your child will be more likely to cooperate with you if he is treated kindly.

The best way to get respectful treatment from your child is to treat him respectfully.

Have Two-Way Conversations

WHEN RESEARCHERS ask children and adolescents to name the things they wish were different about their family life, one of the top things on the list is almost always that they wish their parents would spend more time just talking with them.

If you are just about ready to fall out of your chair after reading this, you're not alone. It comes as a surprise to almost all parents to learn that children wish their parents would talk to them *more*, not less.

Most parents think they already spend plenty of time talking to their child and that the problem is that their child fails to respond or listen to them. Parents frequently complain that when they try to initiate conversations, their child responds with one-word answers: "How was school?" "Fine." "What did you do this afternoon?" "Nothing." "Where are you going?" "Out." As a result, parents believe their children think they talk too much, not too little.

The reason that children and parents have such different perspectives on the issue of communication is that parents don't distinguish between talking *to* their child and talking *with* their child. What feels to parents like a conversation often feels to children like a lecture, a sermon, or an inquisition.

If you were to ask children whether they wished their parents would lecture or cross-examine them more frequently, obviously they'd say no. But if you were to ask children if they wished their parents would converse with them in a way that showed that their parents were really listening, genuinely interested in what they had to say, and willing to engage in a two-way conversation, you'd hear a resounding yes.

Do you talk *to* your child, or *with* your child?

It's easy for parents to fall into the habit of one-way communication that flows from them to their child but not the reverse. Part of your job as a parent is to monitor your child, to teach your child how to do things, and to convey your ideas about what's really important in life. This will naturally require asking questions (to monitor your child, you have to ask who, what, and where), engaging in instruction (to teach your child about the world, you have to explain things), and doing a bit of sermonizing (to help your child acquire the right values, you have to get on your soapbox every once in a while).

There is a big difference, however, between having some of your conversations with your child revolve around monitoring, instructing, or learning life's lessons and having *all* of them be like this. Imagine being in a relationship with someone who is always checking up on you, teaching you, or trying to improve your behavior. Even if that person's intentions are good, a relationship like this will drive you crazy after a while. It's boring and tedious and it makes you feel small and insignificant to always be spoken to by someone who is (or who acts) more powerful, more knowledgeable, or more experienced.

It feels the same way to your child when you always talk *to* her rather than *with* her.

We all want others to care about us, help us, and inspire us (which presumably is why parents ask a lot of questions and deliver a lot of lectures). But we want other things as well when we have conversations. We want to have our chance to be heard. We want to have our point of view valued, not just corrected. We want to have opportunities to teach as well as learn and to exchange information that doesn't entail a right or wrong answer.

When you and your child are talking, try to have a real conversation that is based on two-way communication. It doesn't matter how young your child is. She needs only to be three to be able to engage in verbal give-and-take.

To have two-way conversations with your child, you need to adopt the right attitude and develop certain communication techniques. The techniques are relatively easy to acquire once you have the proper frame of mind, so let's start with that.

The key to developing the sort of attitude that will lead to more and better two-way conversations with your child is accepting that even though you are the authority figure in the relationship you don't always have to assert your authority to maintain it. Asking your child to teach you something doesn't diminish your importance as a teacher; it shows that you are willing to learn as well as instruct. Soliciting your child's opinion about a decision the two of you are discussing doesn't mean that his view will carry the day; it demonstrates that you are open to being influenced by what he thinks. Asking your child what she thinks about something she's read, heard, or seen doesn't mean that you've lost the ability to shape her views; it shows that you are interested in what she has to say.

Once you are comfortable with this attitude, you can start to employ the tools that experts have found contribute to better two-way communication between parents and children.

First and foremost, *pay attention*. I can't stress this enough. You can't engage in a two-way conversation if you pay attention only when you are doing the talking. Concentrate on what your child is saying. Use nonverbal communication to show you are genuinely interested (put the newspaper down, make eye contact, and lean forward). Let your child feel that what she has to say is important and interesting. If it's important to her, it should be important to you.

Second, *actively solicit your child's viewpoint*. Don't always wait for your child to weigh in; ask her what she thinks about things. If you've just described a couple of alternatives for the family's summer vacation, ask her opinion. If you saw something on the news that might be of interest to her, describe it and then ask what she thinks. If something happened to you at work that is worth relating, don't just tell the story. Ask your child what she thinks, what she would have done, and so on.

Third, *ask questions that call for detailed responses rather than one-word answers*. You can't have a two-way conversation with someone if there's nothing to converse about. Instead of asking whether she liked the book you've just finished reading to her (which will probably get you a simple yes or no), ask *what* she liked (or didn't like) about it. Specific questions ("What did your teacher say about your science project?") work better than general ones ("How was science today?").

Fourth, *don't interrupt*. Let your child have a chance to finish what he wants to say. Children take longer than adults to articulate their thoughts and feelings. Don't jump in and finish your child's sentences for him, even if you get the gist of what he's trying to say. Be patient. It's not unusual for a child to give a long-winded answer to what you think is a simple question. You ask what happened in school, hoping to hear about what he's been learning, and he launches into a ten-minute story about something that occurred during recess. Let him finish his story and wait until later to ask him specifically about what you're interested in. When you cut your child off, you are sending the message that you aren't really interested in what he has to say.

Finally, *be genuine*. Don't ask questions just for the sake of asking them. Your child will give answers just for the sake of answering you. Surely there must be some things about your child's life that you are truly interested in. This goes for your responses as well as your questions. If your child has been talking about a problem, for example, don't respond with empty reassurances ("I'm sure everything will work out just fine"). If what's bothering her is important enough for her to bring up, it warrants a thoughtful response from you.

One-way communication can show your child that you care about her. But a two-way conversation shows both that you care about her and that you respect her.

"Don't Talk Back"

THERE ARE CERTAIN EXPRESSIONS you should eliminate from the repertoire of responses you use when talking to your child, and one of them is "Don't talk back." Other, similar responses to your child's questions or expressions of opinion are "You'll know better when you're older," "If I want your opinion, I'll ask for it," "Keep your mouth shut," and "Children should be seen and not heard."

Promise yourself that you are going to break the habit of using these expressions. I know you don't always have time for a debate or discussion, but there are more polite ways of telling your child that you are making a preemptive decision than telling him that what he thinks doesn't matter, that his youth automatically makes what he thinks irrelevant, or that he should play dead and roll over whenever someone older or more powerful asks him to do something.

If you treat your child with respect and consider his opinions most of the time, he will come to understand that inevitably there will be situations in which you are going to have to use your best judgment and make your best decision, even if this means he will not get his way. This might occur when you are in a hurry, when a decision is more complicated than a child his age can really comprehend, when you are too stressed out by other things to have the patience for a long, drawn-out argument, and when you're sure you're correct and have tried your best to explain your reasoning.

The best thing to do in these situations is to calmly and politely explain why you cannot, or will not, change your mind.

Here are some ways to say "I'm going to use my authority as a parent to have the final word" in a way that shows consideration and respect for your child. Try some of them (just make sure that you adapt the wording to suit your child's age):

"I hear what you're saying, and I've done my best to explain how I feel, but I think we just disagree. I'm just going to have use my best judgment." (Saying that you considered your child's opinion but disagree with it is different from saying that he's not entitled to have a point of view.)

"I need to decide this in a hurry and don't have time to discuss it right now. Let's do it my way now, and then talk about it later so that the next time the situation comes up, I'll have a better understanding of what your opinion is." (Saying that your concern now is time pressure leaves open the possibility that you might make a different decision the next time.)

"I know we disagree, but the situation is a lot more complicated than I think you understand. Let's remember to talk about it later

so that I can explain some of the different aspects of it to you."
(Saying that a decision may require more knowledge, information,
or experience than your child has is not the same as saying that his
youth alone disqualifies him, because it stresses that the issue is
expertise—which makes sense—not age—which doesn't.)

"I've had a really bad day [or am under a lot of pressure at
work, or have a bad headache, or whatever]. It would help me a
lot if you would look at this from my point of view and go along
with what I want." (Allowing your child to feel helpful by cooper-
ating may diffuse the tension over your disagreement. It also says
that under other circumstances, you might decide things differently.)

When all else fails, you can also try humor. A friend of mine
once told me that his father used to say, "Everyone is entitled to
his own ignorant opinion, and you are certainly entitled to yours."
Just make sure your child knows you are kidding around and using
humor to avoid a prolonged argument.

The problem with "Don't talk back" and its variants is that
they are blanket statements that mean disagreeing with someone
is bad or disrespectful. This is not what you want to teach your
child. You want your child to understand that reasonable people
can disagree and discuss their disagreements respectfully.

Let Your Child Act His Age

PART OF RESPECTING your child as a person involves allowing
your child to act his age. This requires enjoying the stage of development your child is going through right now and resisting the
temptation to help push him into the next one. Let his development unfold without trying to direct it all the time.

It's natural to want to structure your child's life so that she's on
a pathway toward happiness and success. But parenting is only
partly about preparing your child for what will come in the future.

It's also about seeing that your child enjoys life in the present. Allow your child to act her age. She will grow up faster than you think without your doing anything to make it happen.

Your infant will wean herself, learn how to use a spoon, walk, start using language, and learn toilet training just fine without your trying to move things along on what you think the "right" schedule is. Children develop at different rates, and they can be advanced in one realm (for instance, motor development) but slower in others (for instance, language). Let your child develop at her own speed. If you are worried that your child is developing too slowly during infancy or any other stage, check with your pediatrician. Usually you'll learn that you have nothing to worry about.

Allow your toddler to learn about the world by letting him discover what's around him. Don't worry about deliberately preparing him for preschool; he will learn what he needs to know without any special teaching from you. Your two-year-old doesn't need flash cards to stimulate his intellectual development. What he needs most at this point is a safe environment he can explore and parents who are happy to get down on the floor and play with him just for the fun of it. Don't turn each interaction with him into a lesson. He will learn plenty from you if you read to him every day and spend enough quality time with him.

Don't force your preschooler to act like a grown-up. Four-year-olds can be loud, messy, boisterous, inattentive, and silly. You'll have a better and easier time as a parent if you go along for the ride and allow yourself to be playful, messy, and silly with her. Being a child is supposed to be fun. She'll have plenty of pressure on her to be serious and disciplined when she's older. For now, let her act like a preschooler instead of forcing her to be four going on forty.

Make sure you allow your elementary school child enough time to play. Don't overschedule his days with lessons, tutors, and personal coaches. It's great to be able to play the violin, tap dance, and hit a cross-court forehand with topspin. But it's also great to know how to relax, how to entertain oneself, and how to do absolutely, positively nothing. Try to strike a balance between structured and unstructured activities. A nine-year-old's life should not be a nonstop academy.

Let your teenager enjoy being an adolescent. Helping her gradually mature into adulthood is fine; insisting that she act like an adult when she is only thirteen is not. It's normal for teenagers to get carried away, to be wild from time to time, to overdo things, to experiment, and to live for the moment. Your job as a parent is not to stifle these tendencies, but to do your best to see that she is protected from harm along the way.

Don't be in such a hurry to have your child finish one stage of development and move on to the next. Childhood is not a race to see who gets to adulthood first.

Children Treat Others the Way Their Parents Treat Them

YOUR RELATIONSHIP WITH your child is the foundation for her relationships with others. If you treat your child with compassion, kindness, and respect, she will grow up to be a concerned, caring, and considerate person. If you are uncaring, aloof, and dismissive, that's how she's likely to turn out when she grows up.

It's not that individuals who receive less than optimal parenting are automatically doomed to repeat their parents' mistakes. It's just that what comes naturally to people who were raised in an environment that was loving, firm, and respectful takes a lot of effort for those whose parents were harsh, indifferent, or insensitive. It's certainly possible to overcome a difficult childhood, but it isn't easy. Our gut response is to treat people the way we ourselves were treated when we were raised, so any about-face has to be conscious, deliberate, and effortful.

In other words, if you treat your child with respect, you will make the rest of his life a whole lot easier. He'll find it easier to make friends. He'll find it easier to be successful in school and at work. He'll find it easier to have a happy marriage. He'll find it easier to be a better parent to his own children.

Nothing can guarantee that anyone will have good friendships, satisfying romances, a successful career, and a happy family life. But being raised in a home in which you are loved, guided, and respected dramatically increases the odds of all of these things. This isn't a matter of debate. It's a proven fact.

I'm sure you know people who were raised by nasty, uncaring, or indifferent parents but who nevertheless turned out to be warm, sensitive, and compassionate. All I can say is that these people are lucky exceptions to a well-established general rule. Don't trust your child's emotional future to luck.

It's been said that "It takes a village to raise a child," but the fact is that most children are raised by their parents, not by a village. In the search for what helps children grow up to be healthy, happy, and successful, we have yet to discover anything that compares to having good parents who love, guide, and respect their children.

There is no more important job in any society than raising children, and there is no more important influence on how children develop than their parents.

Index